C000064823

PRETTY BOY
DVD EDITION

ROY SHAW

JOHN BLAKE

Published by John Blake Publishing Ltd,
3 Bramber Court, 2 Bramber Road,
London W14 9PB, England

www.blake.co.uk

First published in hardback in 2007

ISBN: 978-1-84454-289-5

All rights reserved. No part of this publication may be reproduced, stored in a
retrieval system, or in any form or by any means, without the prior permission in
writing of the publisher, nor be otherwise circulated in any form of binding or
cover other than that in which it is published and without a similar condition
including this condition being imposed on the subsequent publisher.

British Library Cataloguing-in-Publication Data:

A catalogue record for this book is available from the British Library.

Design by www.envydesign.co.uk

Printed in Great Britain by William Clowes Ltd, Beccles, Suffolk

1 3 5 7 9 10 8 6 4 2

© Text copyright Roy Shaw/Kate Kray 2007

Papers used by John Blake Publishing are natural, recyclable products made
from wood grown in sustainable forests. The manufacturing processes conform
to the environmental regulations of the country of origin.

Every attempt has been made to contact the relevant copyright-holders,
but some were unobtainable. We would be grateful if the appropriate
people could contact us.

DEDICATED TO ALL THE FRIENDS
WHO HAVE STOOD BESIDE ME THROUGH
THICK AND THIN.

CONTENTS

BOXING at CINATRA'S

CROYDON

MONDAY 10TH APRIL

E. Hamid presents:

IN AID OF THE

FREDDI MILL'S

BOY'S CLUB

FOR

HANDICAPPED

CHILDREN

ROY (PRETTY BOY)

SHAW

DAGENHAM

Vs.

LENNY

McLEAN

HOXTON

STEVE (COLOMBO) RICHARD
Vs
PAT MORRISSON IRELAND

PATSY GUTTERIDGE
Vs
DANNY CHIPPENDALE

PLUS FULL SUPPORTING CONTESTS

Doors Open at 7 p.m.

Boxing Commences at 8 p.m

Tickets Available from:

JOE PYLE 703 9702
MICK SAVAGE 22 48741
PAT CAHILL 474 4733

TED ONSLOW 599 0691
ALEC STEENE 839 5363
(THE BULL,) ROMFORD MARKET

Ticket Prices at £12.50, £10.00, £7.50, £7.00

ACKNOWLEDGEMENTS

Ray Mills – who supported and visited me throughout my prison years.

Bertie Costa – who stood like a man when we were tried for murder.

Barbara – who helped open my eyes when I was released from prison.

Eric Warne – we were pals since school.

Joe Carrington – who promoted my last three fights.

Sharon – my former girlfriend and still a friend.

Terry Garwood – computer wizard.

Freda Bolton – for all her hard work and dedication.

Bobby Reading, John Sabeani, Patsy Gutteridge, Micky May, Colombo, Math twins, Paul Whitworth, Charlie Bronson, Danny Chippendale, Joe Lazarous, Bobby Howes, Rod 'John Conteh look-alike'.

I would also like to thank all my friends in and out of prison who supported me throughout my boxing career, there are too many to mention by name but I would like to ask them just one more favour: BUY MY BOOK ... OR ELSE!

UPDATE TO THIS EDITION

My publisher asked to me to write an update on Roy 'Pretty Boy' Shaw for the release of his forthcoming book, aptly named *Pretty Boy*. I made a cup of tea, sat at my computer, scratched my head and wracked my brain. What was there to say about the formidable Mr Shaw going into 2008? Is he married? Is he financially secure? Is he perhaps a little wiser? More settled? Mellowed with age? Mmmm...

OK, OK, Ok – here's the update. The point is, there is no update! Well, not much to speak of anyway. Roy still goes out on the town on three-day benders, he is still looking for love, he is several millions richer – straight money, of course! Older, definitely; wiser, maybe. Mellowed, don't make me laugh! He still has his ferocious temper and, yes, if you take a liberty with him he will fucking kill you.

Anything else? Nah, I don't think so. I think that's just about everything...

Kate Kray, 2007

INTRODUCTION

I ARRIVED AT THE HOME OF ROY SHAW, known as the hardest man in England, on a hot summer day. I looked around at the security protecting his property; closed-circuit cameras monitored my every move. I pressed a small buzzer and waited. Almost immediately, a voice growled over the intercom, 'Who is it?'

I waved into the security camera and smiled. 'It's me, Kate Kray.'

The heavily barred electric gates swept majestically open to let me through. Standing on the driveway was a shiny red Bentley Corniche with a personalised number plate. Next to it was a royal blue Mercedes sports. If that doesn't just about say it all, then what does?

Although this was the first time I'd been to Roy Shaw's home, we'd met before on 6 November 1989. The reason the date is so prominent in my mind is because it was the day I married Ronnie Kray, and was the day I was introduced to Ron's world – the underworld.

Each and every one of the 200 guests dressed in wide-shouldered suits introduced themselves to me in turn. I met them all – hoodlums, bank robbers, enforcers, murderers – but one man who introduced himself was different from the rest, I could feel it the moment I met him. His name was Roy Shaw. I knew instantly he was a formidable man, extremely menacing and very, very dangerous.

We met on the odd occasion at benefit nights laid on by

gangsters for gangsters who were doing time. I never got into an in-depth conversation with Roy, it was more a case of a kiss on the cheek, a hug and 'How's the Colonel?'

The last time I saw Roy was at my husband's funeral in March 1995. On that sad day, there were over 50,000 mourners pushing and shoving for a better view of the cortége. Security was tight, and amid the mayhem I noticed Roy Shaw pull up in his Bentley alone. He got out and was dressed in an irridescent electric-blue suit. He straightened his tie and walked towards a wall of security men. As he approached, they stepped back, parting like the Red Sea to let him through. Not one of them challenged him – they daren't.

Three years on, I arrived at his home to interview him for a book I was in the middle of researching about the toughest men in the country. As he showed me into his lounge on that hot, sunny afternoon, I sat on his sofa and sipped an ice-cold drink and listened as he started to unravel his harrowing life story. The more I listened, I became convinced that Roy Shaw was a cut above the rest in the violent dog-eat-dog world in which he lived.

It was a story that needed to be told, and within a week the contracts were signed and I began to write Roy's story as he told it.

As each day, and then each week passed, and as the interviews progressed, we slowly peeled away the layers that Roy had built up over the years to protect himself. There was layer upon layer of madness, sadness, indifference, hate and, most of all, anger, that needed to be resolved. Roy went through the gamut of emotions, reliving the highs and lows of his life. He laughed at times, and cried, and was embarrassed by neither.

As we stripped away the protective shell, for the first time in his life Roy bared his soul. There were times when he had difficulty in expressing himself, and understanding why he was such a violent, angry young man.

But that's just it – there were no reasons. I would like to be able to say he was so violent because of something specific, an underlying problem or a justifiable motive – but I can't. There is no justification, none whatsoever, for Roy's violence, and he would agree. He doesn't blame his childhood or society, and doesn't try to avoid the truth, because the buck stops with him. Roy laid down his own boundaries for himself and never overstepped the invisible mark, or allowed anyone else to. He has his own priorities which have made him strong, and he has examined his own experiences, good and bad, very carefully, and learned from them.

Every Wednesday and Friday I visited Roy at his luxurious home in Essex. He was always ready and waiting for me with a smile. His greeting was always the same, warm and sincere, but looking into Roy's face, and particularly deep into his eyes, Roy's unique character blazed through. I've said it before and I'll say it again, his eyes are cold and expressionless, and would look more at home on a great white man-eating shark. They're small and are closely set above a corrugated nose. Roy appears to stare with an unnerving intensity into a secret world of hostility and hatred.

Everything about Roy spells violence. His shoulders start underneath his chin and spread outwards like a rugged mountain. Touch him and he feels like a rock. He is 15 stone of squat, solid muscle which knots and bulges under his silk shirt when he moves. How he looks, and how he actually is, I found to be a contradiction in itself.

Roy is always a pleasure to be with. He has endearing qualities that, for whatever reason, men of today rarely possess. He is one of the old school, and knows how to treat a lady. He would open doors and step back to let me through, take my coat for me, watch his Ps and Qs in order not to offend me, because it's not tough or clever to be uncouth. In short, he's a true gentleman.

The first day I interviewed Roy, he asked me what I liked to drink. From then on, he always added it to his shopping list. Somehow, I always had trouble imagining Roy Shaw pushing a shopping trolley around Marks & Spencers. But he does. Every week. And each time, he'd buy me something special – a cherry or a chocolate cake – which he'd serve on a monogrammed tea plate with the initials 'RS' emblazoned on the edge in gold.

I teased him one day by asking him if he'd stayed at the Royal Swallow hotel. He laughed and told me not to be saucy. You only have to scratch the surface to discover that Roy has a dry sense of humour, like the time when he told me he had bought a memory book. When I asked him why he'd bought a memory book, he said that he'd become quite forgetful. He added that it had cost him about £200. I asked to see the book, particularly as it had cost a small fortune, but he shrugged, laughed, and said he'd forgotten where he'd put it. We shared a number of these light-hearted moments while writing his chilling and disturbing story.

Initially, Roy found it difficult talking about himself. He was shy and awkward with me, but after a couple of visits he relaxed and started to open up. He'd protected himself for so long and had never let anyone get close, or see him vulnerable and exposed.

As we were writing this book, he regressed back to childhood and relived every moment, and while talking we stumbled across what I believe to be the trigger for Roy's deep-rooted anger.

He was badly bullied as a boy, and his father was killed when he was ten. That's when he had his heart ripped out, leaving him, as some would say, heartless. Roy never dealt with his grief, and from that day on, he pulled up the shutters, battened down the hatches, and cocooned himself in his own world, never allowing himself to be hurt again.

Word on the street soon spread that I was writing Roy's biography, and everyone had their own story to tell about him, each tale more violent than the last. After describing each violent episode in minute detail, most would whisper, 'But don't tell Roy I told you.'

I have written five crime books and I write regularly for a crime magazine, so no amount of violence fazes me. I've become hardened to it. It's true of most cases I've researched that there are usually only one or two incidents in a book around which everything else revolves; the rest is descriptive colour, or padding. What makes Roy Shaw's story different is that no padding was required. In fact, I had to water down instances of sheer brutality because I don't believe in writing about violence for violence's sake.

Boys will be boys and men will be men. They all like to poke fires, chase girls and fight. If the truth be told, the majority of men only fight once in a blue moon, if at all. Roy has had a fight almost every day of his life. It comes as naturally to him as breathing.

What is missing from this book, because words do not do them justice, are Roy's many gestures. On numerous occasions during our conversations, he'd leap up from his seat and demonstrate with clenched fists exactly how he'd whacked someone, or emphasise the venomous thrust when stabbing a victim. But he never did this to brag or show off. It was simply so I could get it exactly right. It was then I saw Roy Shaw come alive when he re-enacted his many murderous acts.

Roy says he is a businessman now and has retired from his profession – violence. The word 'retirement' is not applicable to men like Roy; it's more suited to accountants or lawyers. Gangsters don't retire – they're more like legendary cowboys, slowly fading away into the background, because you can never retire from what or who you really are. Roy Shaw is an enforcer and always will be.

At the end of writing this book, I asked Roy if there was anything he wanted to say to the men he'd hurt or the boxers he'd punished in the ring. Perhaps he'd like to take the opportunity for a word or two of regret, explanation or apology? Roy pondered on that thought. I looked into his piercing blue eyes, waiting for some words of wisdom:

'Mmm .. yeah ...' he nodded. 'Fuck 'em.'

Kate Kray,

FOREWORD

I'M KNOWN AS A RUTHLESS BASTARD and I am a ruthless bastard. The whole of my life has been fight, fight, fight. It's what I am, a fighter. Some people can talk their way out of a problem, while others manipulate or buy their way out. Me – I fight my way out.

I didn't set out to get a reputation, that was never my intention. I didn't suddenly wake up one morning and decide on a life of crime, it just crept up on me and before I knew it, I was a ruthless bastard. I admit I enjoy the respect shown to me because of my reputation. Writing this book has made me think that maybe the respect I thought I'd earned was shown to me because I demanded it through fear. There is a fine line between the two and it's only now I realise the difference between earning respect and demanding it.

I've never thought about writing my autobiography. In fact, it never entered my head until a funny little blonde sort called Kate Kray asked me. Kate phoned and arranged to visit me because of some book research she was doing.

I agreed and before I had the chance to change my mind, Kate had dotted the 'I's and crossed the 'T's and my signature was on the contract.

At first, I found it difficult to talk about my life, as I've never been able to confide in anyone. Even at the best of times, I find it difficult to express myself and my innermost feelings.

I've never been able to understand the reasons why I was so violent and, to be honest, I still don't fully understand it. But when you're forced to analyse yourself and look deeper, you find answers, even though you've never asked the questions.

I don't regret the life I've led, not for one moment. We're all in charge of our own destiny, I just regret wasting all that time behind bars, because you only have one life and shouldn't waste a moment of it because you will never get out of it alive.

One of the reasons I agreed to write this book is this: if it helps stop one young tearaway, just one, from going down the road I went down, then it would all be worthwhile. It would be my way of putting something back into society instead of taking it out.

If I can pass on anything from my experiences to a young up-and-coming villain, it's this: you gain very little, but lose so much, by trying to be something you're not.

Some things are precious and should be guarded and cherished at whatever cost, like freedom, love and life. I lost my freedom for 15 years in prison, I lost the loves of my life through my inability to conform, and I've taken life with a total disregard for anyone.

I can categorically state that it's not big and it's not clever to go to prison. I'm not going to preach or stand on a soapbox, patronising youngsters by telling them not to commit crime. I can't offer them any words of wisdom, just the benefit of my own experiences. But at the end of the day, it's their decision, and theirs alone.

There are only three possible outcomes which you should be aware of before embarking on a life of crime, and it doesn't matter who you are or who you think you are, nobody, and I mean nobody, is untouchable. Make no mistake, if you choose the road I walked down, then you will suffer one of these three consequences:

ONE
The most likely. You'll spend the best part of your life languishing in a stinking prison cell, surrounded by two-bob drug dealers, paedophiles and, your worst nightmare, the prison queens.

TWO

A possibility. You'd better hope and pray to God that you never end up rotting in the dungeons of Broadmoor, pumped full of drugs, dribbling at the mouth, and listening to the haunting cries of lunatics locked in padded cells.

THREE

Always remember there are no rules on the street, and it's highly likely you'll end up dead in a lonely country lane with a bullet in the head.

I've told you what will happen – the choice is yours. My advice is free, take it or leave it. I survived, but only just ...

CHAPTER 1

GIFT FROM GOD

'That was the first time I felt the adrenalin rush.
It started with a tingle in my feet. The anger welled up
through my body like an electric current. In a flash,
I felt I had the strength of ten men. It was such a high.
I lashed out. BANG ...'

'THERE'S SHAW.'

I looked round. Four boys were running towards me.

'Get him,' they yelled.

It was the bullies. I ran as fast as I could across the school playground. Every day was the same. I knew what was coming. I was scared – bloody scared. My heart started to pound faster and faster. The harder I ran, the faster it beat. Again, I glanced over my shoulder. As I turned back, two more boys appeared from behind a wall directly in front of me. One of them grabbed me.

'Let me go, let me go,' I shouted.

They started to laugh. The other boys who'd been chasing me caught up. All of them circled me, laughing and jeering. I felt helpless. Scared.

'Leave me alone,' I yelled.

One of them shoved me hard in the back. I banged my head as I hit the ground. I pleaded with them to stop but they didn't listen. I felt a hard blow to the back of my head as one of the bullies screamed, 'Shut the fuck up.'

I struggled and struggled, trying to break free, but it was no good. Suddenly, they all started punching and kicking me. Blows rained down on me from every angle.

Instinctively, I curled into a ball while they bashed me. That's how it was throughout my school years. I was taunted and bullied relentlessly. I don't know the reason why I was picked on; maybe it was because I was small for my age, or because I was a loner. Who knows?

One thing's for sure – I dreaded the sound of the school bell. To a child, the future is the next five seconds and a day seems like a lifetime. I was kicked and punched through the infant and junior school. In retrospect, five years of being bullied seemed an eternity and, at times, I hated the world for being born.

I was born in Stepney, East London, on 11 March 1936, within the sound of Bow Bells. I'm a true cockney, a Londoner through and through. It was the calm before the storm, three years before the Second World War started.

London was a great place to live; it was a time of ease and peace. The only force to be reckoned with were East End women, who were all gas and garters, wearing paisley pinnies with a no-nonsense look on their faces and a Woodbine cigarette hanging from the corner of their mouths. They were found daily, on hands and knees frantically scrubbing their doorsteps as though it was the only thing that mattered, or leaning over the garden fence discussing Mrs What's-Her-Name at Number 43: ' 'Ere ... you know her lodger ... ?'

Us kids played nearby in relative safety. I was a street urchin, a ragamuffin searching the pavements for dog-ends, using the extra tobacco to make roll-ups for my dad.

Times were hard – we didn't have much but we were happy and content, unaware of what was ahead of us. No one could have foreseen that Hitler was about to invade Poland and every Londoner's life would change for ever.

I was just six years old when I was evacuated to the country – Chippenham in Wiltshire – with my three sisters and my mum. We were lucky because we were packed off together as a family and I was delighted when I arrived at the rambling farm and saw two beautiful Labrador dogs. From the day I arrived, they became my best friends and the memories of those dogs remain with me to this day.

Wiltshire was different to London – bigger, cleaner, quieter. There were many farms, huge country houses and sprawling open fields, which I would run through with the two dogs for hours. When it started to get dark, Mum would send out a search party. Often I could be found with my gas mask and two knackered dogs slumped under a tree fast asleep. Mum never knew whether to kiss me or scold me.

We returned home from Wiltshire before the war had ended. The devastation in London was obvious, even to me. Complete areas of East London were flattened, reduced to rubble. Whole communities were moved out of the city and into the sticks; we were moved to a house in Dagenham which had a back garden. My first reaction was 'Great, a garden ... I can have a dog.' I badgered Mum and Dad. I kept on and on about a dog. Dad had other ideas – a vegetable plot. I hated that garden plot; Dad made me pick up all the stones if I was naughty.

After the war, Dad was de-mobbed, and worked as a lorry driver for a timber yard and often brought home the excess wood to sell.

Half of the garden was taken up with his prize lettuces and the other half was used for chopping firewood to make into bundles and sell round the houses for extra money. I would spend hours in the backyard helping Dad. Whenever I asked for a dog he would wink and say, 'We'll see. Let's get this wood chopped and sold first, then maybe.' I never did get the dog.

Dad had two passions in his life – his garden and speedway racing, although motorbikes were his first passion. I would sit on an upturned bucket next to him for hours while he fiddled with a motorbike engine. I was Dad's little helper. I went with him to every race meeting on the back of his bike, holding on tightly round his waist. He would watch me in the wing mirror as my lips contorted uncontrollably in the wind and he would laugh.

It was a hot afternoon on the last day of July. As usual, I was pottering round the garden with Dad. There was a big race meeting that night at West Ham speedway and I was excited about going. Jock, our lodger, came into the garden for a smoke and started chatting with Dad about the bike.

'I wouldn't mind going with you tonight,' Jock said. 'Perhaps we'll have a pint afterwards.'

As soon as he said the word 'pint' I knew I wouldn't be going. I was disappointed. I desperately wanted to go and protested.

'But, Dad ...'

Dad threw me a look. 'You can come another time.'

It was all arranged. Jock was going and I wasn't. For the rest of the day, I slumped around the house sulking. I kept looking at Dad with big cow eyes hoping he would change his mind. I even followed him to the bathroom and watched him shave. When it was time for him to go, I got his crash helmet and gloves from the cupboard under the stairs and handed them to him with my head bowed. I didn't speak. I couldn't look at him. Dad, realising I was so disappointed, pulled on a big leather glove and ruffled my hair, trying to make me laugh. He pointed to the ceiling and said, 'What's that up there?'

Instinctively, I looked up. He tickled me in the ribs and teased, 'Caught you out there.' I squealed with laughter as Dad slammed the door behind him.

That was the last time I ever saw my dad alive. I was ten years old. Later that night, the police came. I was lying in bed when I heard Mum scream. My older sisters looked after me while Mum went to the hospital. When she came back, her face was ashen. She sat me down on the sofa; her eyes were red and puffy.

'Daddy's dead,' she whispered.

At first, I couldn't take it in.

'Daddy's dead?' I repeated.

There had been a terrible accident on the way home from the speedway track. A lorry had swerved out of control. One of the pedals on the motorbike hit the kerb. Jock had been thrown clear. Dad tried to regain control of his bike, but it was no good. He hit a lamppost head on and was killed instantly. It must have been fate that he didn't take me with him that night.

Over the following week, I wandered about in a dream. I didn't cry, not once. At night, I lay in bed listening to my mum and sisters weeping into their pillows. I couldn't believe Dad was dead; it was so unreal.

On the day Dad was buried, there was a lot of activity in the house and far-flung relatives wearing black arm bands arrived. I sat on the sideboard watching it all. I watched them slide Dad's coffin into the back of the hearse and Mum putting on her best black coat.

'Where's my Roy?' she called out.

Mum looked round the room and saw me sitting on the sideboard. She smiled a beautiful smile full of reassurance and love. Her motherly instinct was to make me look right, so she spat on the corner of her handkerchief and wiped the dirt off my face, as if it mattered.

I sat in the church and played with my toy motorbike, the one Dad had given me. I didn't take in what was going on until we stood round the freshly dug grave. The vicar stood at one end. 'Ashes to ashes, dust to dust ...'

They started to lower the oak coffin into the ground and it hit me like a ton of bricks. That was my dad they were putting into the ground. I shrieked at the top of my voice, 'Don't go, Dad,' and hurled myself on top of the coffin. My uncles grabbed my legs. 'Come on, Roy, you'll be all right.'

I held on to my father's coffin for dear life. I didn't want to let him go. I didn't want him to be in that cold grave on his own. Who would I go to speedway with? Who would cut my hair? Who would help me chop the wood? In that moment I realised I would never see my dad again.

Three days later I was back at school and back to the bullies. The bell rang sounding the end of the school day. I bolted out of the classroom eager to get home. For a change, I managed to get through the main gates with no one chasing me. I breathed a sigh of relief, loosened my tie, took off my blazer and wondered what was for tea. I looked up and, to my horror, standing directly ahead of me were eight boys. The bullies. I turned and ran in the opposite direction, my fear giving me extra speed. But it was no good, two more were waiting to ambush me. I was scared. My heart was pounding like a runaway train and my chest heaved as I struggled to gulp in air as they grabbed me. But this time when the bullies circled me, I felt different. Strange. I was still frightened but my fear turned to anger. An anger so deep inside of me it erupted. I was angry that my dad had died and left me, angry because one minute I was sitting on an upturned bucket next to Dad and the next minute he was gone. Where? Why? A million questions ran through my mind. Now the bullies wanted to take things from me, too; well, I had nothing left to give. I was angry. Fucking angry. I felt it was me against the whole male world.

That was the first time I felt the adrenalin rush. It started with a tingle in my feet. The anger welled up through my body like an electric current. In a flash, I felt I had the strength of ten men. It was such a high. I lashed out. BANG. I hit one of the bullies on the chin. He went over. Then another. Then another. I felt the anger and frustration come out in those first few punches.

I found a strength I never knew I had. I lashed out for all the times the bullies had taunted me, all the times I had been frightened, all the times I'd been hurt and, from that day on, I realised that bullies are cowards, and if you hurt a coward they cry the loudest. I started to whack the bullies and anyone else who stood in my way. God had given me a gift. I lost my fear and gained a power. I knew I was never going to be frightened or ever run away again. From that day on, I moved slowly, 'cos I didn't have to move for anyone.

I started to do well at school. My dad's brother, Uncle Alf, took me under his wing. Alf was a big man with thick ginger hair that was cut in an old-fashioned pudding basin style. Dad had four brothers, all tough, hard-working men. Alfie was into boxing in a big way and took me to the local boxing booth held on the bombed-out site in Commercial Road, Stepney. There, anyone could challenge anyone for a fight. The first time I went, my uncle shadow boxed around me, ducking and weaving, tapping my cheeks and teasing me: 'So you think you can hold your hands up, boy?'

I laughed. 'Yeah, I'll have a tear-up.'

Uncle Alf grinned, then disappeared for a while. He came back chatting to a man with a towel around his neck and holding a bucket.

'Come on then, son,' the man said, 'let's see what you can do.'

I followed him into a huge circus tent, which held a boxing ring. Two boxers were slugging it out. Spectators were shouting, 'Go on, knock 'im out.'

I was led into a makeshift dressing room to get ready, but I didn't have anything to wear except my swimming trunks, because earlier that day I'd been swimming with my sister. I unrolled the damp towel and to my horror I saw a girl's green seersucker swimming costume and a rubber swimming hat. I looked at the trainer. He tutted, spat on the floor, sniffed and growled, 'Get it on.'

I was a bit nervous as I climbed into the ring. I saw my opponent standing in his corner warming up. He was wearing a long silk dressing gown, proper shorts and boots. He was on his toes, dancing like a pro. He looked at me and smirked. There I was, a skinny kid, wearing my sister's tucked down swimming costume as shorts, plimsolls and a pair of big brown leather boxing gloves. They were huge, as big as my head and still damp inside, from the sweat of the previous fighter.

I looked at my corner to the man with the bucket. I don't know why, maybe for reassurance.

'Use yer jab, kid. Look busy. Move about and jab,' he hissed.

Before I could answer the bell rang. DING DING.

My opponent rushed at me, bobbing and weaving. I stood in the middle of the ring holding my hands up. The fucking gloves were so big I could barely see over the top of them. He was boxing clever, and kept jabbing me. I couldn't catch him because of my inexperience. Then he caught me with a good punch. In that moment, I had a flash-back to the playground bullies. I felt the anger, the adrenalin rush.

Then he made a fatal mistake and stepped within my reach. I let the big one go. BANG. He was on his arse. All I could see over the top of my gloves were the soles of his feet. The crowd erupted. Uncle Alf went wild. After that fight, I can't remember a single fight when I was frightened.

That day I won £3 in the boxing booth. Uncle Alf realised my potential and urged me to take up boxing. I started training, and boxing became my life. By the time I was 16, I'd won the Area Championship, the Essex Championship and the Schoolboy Championship trophies which were held at the Albert Hall. Winning all the trophies boosted my confidence. I'd found the one thing I was good at – boxing – and through that I earned respect, and I liked that.

Respect and trophies were one thing but I had to earn money. So every week I continued to go to the boxing booth with Uncle Alf to put some money in my pocket. In fact, he took me to any boxing show he could, anywhere to earn cash, even a police show. The place was full of Old Bill. My uncle hated them, and knew it would be the only chance I'd get to knock out a policeman legally.

'Make me proud, son. Knock his fucking head off,' he laughed.

I took great delight in doing just that.

Mum got me my first job working with her in a factory as a machinist making ladies' dresses. There were only three other men there: the manager, the cutter and the presser. The rest were all women, a gaggle of loud, mouthy factory girls, all turbans and curlers. And I was a shy, awkward boy who'd never had a girlfriend.

The women sensed this and teased me relentlessly.

'Royston, come 'ere me little darling.'

I dreaded going to work. I'd hide behind the presses and listen to them gossiping. All I wanted to do was training and boxing. I was boxing crazy. I hated that fucking factory and I hated those fucking women. I'd rather have had ten rounds in a boxing ring than ten minutes with them.

I left the dress factory because I was boxing mad and I wanted to concentrate on becoming stronger and fitter. I got a job in a timber yard in Canning Town. I was 16 years old and weighed seven stone. From day one, I felt the other men in the timber yard didn't like me. They'd sneer and say, 'Bloody boys taking our jobs.' They did their best to point out that I wasn't good enough for the job, but I wanted to prove them wrong.

The barges laden with logs came up the river into Silver Town and Canning Town. My job was to carry each log on my back from the barges, walking along a 20ft plank which was only about 12in wide and 3in thick. Walking the plank, which linked the barge to the river bank, was a question of controlled balance. Two men would hold the log up while I got underneath it. If there was a heavy wind, I had to take care not to be blown into the river. It was bloody hard work, and the men used to try to break me by giving me the heaviest logs, but it was a matter of pride and I wouldn't give in. At the end of the day, my back ached. When I first started the job, I'd go home and my back would be raw even to the point of bleeding. Mum bathed my sore back and urged me to pack the job in, but nothing would deter me.

At the same time, I continued with my boxing. I was never too exhausted for a fight. I persevered with my job, gained the respect of the other men and earned a good living. I took home £10 per week, which compared with my uncle who worked as a chauffeur and earned £7, and had a family to support. But best of all, I was growing in strength by the day, and was no longer a seven-stone boy with a good punch – I'd matured into an 18-year-old man with one hell of a punch.

CHAPTER 2

A MEANS TO AN END

'I felt the adrenalin rush. It flared up inside me, starting from my feet, and surged throughout my body making me feel ten times stronger. There was a banging in my head this was no headache, it was an anger so raw, so uncontrollable, it erupted in violence ...'

I N THE LATE SUMMER OF 1954, my letter of conscription into the army fell through the letterbox. I was called up to fight for Queen and Country. Some men dreaded National Service, but I had actually been looking forward to joining the Army. It couldn't have been better for me because I was already training hard for my boxing and I knew the training in the Army would be even harder, but would be something I'd enjoy.

I arrived at the Army Medical Centre full of confidence. I didn't think there would be any problem passing the medical. I was young and fit. I stood in line with the other conscripts, everyone in our birthday suits. Many were trying to get out of being called up by claiming they had flat feet. One even told me he was going to cut off his trigger finger – anything to get out of going. I was the complete opposite; I wasn't looking for any excuses, I wanted to go even to the point of hiding my colour blindness.

The medical officer tapped my chest, I stuck my tongue out when I was told to stick my tongue out and coughed when I was told to cough. I passed the medical with flying colours and was officially 23040113 Private Royston Henry Shaw.

I thought army life was going to be a breeze, just running about all day with a rucksack on my back or in a gymnasium doing press-ups, sit-ups or swinging from ropes. Exercising wasn't a problem, in fact it was perfect for me, but what I didn't reckon on, or could have prepared myself for, was the discipline of being ordered when to sleep, when to eat, when to get up, when to go to bed and even when to have a crap.

The first six weeks in the training camp was a nightmare. I tried hard to tolerate being ordered about because I was learning to drive a three-ton supply lorry, which I enjoyed, but I was finding it increasingly difficult to take the orders that were being barked at me constantly.

The Sergeant was on my back all the time. He was a nasty bully-boy and seemed to be picking on me non-stop. Looking back on it now, he probably didn't, but because of the bullying I'd suffered at school, I felt singled out. I realise now bullies come in all forms throughout life, often in the playground and particularly in the Army, and that Sergeant was the biggest bully I had ever encountered. He would come up close to my ear and bellow at the top of his voice, 'Left, right ... left, right ...'

He did it to all the men. They didn't seem to mind, but I couldn't or wouldn't stand for it. The restrictions, the routine, the very detailed planning of every minute of my day drove me mad. Six weeks of hell and I was just about ready to explode.

It was the crack of dawn. I awoke to a dim morning of overcast skies, and the barracks felt damp. It was a struggle to get out of bed. I shivered and pulled my itchy grey army blanket around me. I longed for five more minutes in bed, just five more minutes in the warm, but it wasn't to be. The Sergeant marched into the barracks with his big shiny boots, squeaking on the highly-polished floor. All the spit and polish in the world would never have got my boots to shine like the Sergeant's. He was like a robot. I don't think that man ever slept, or ate or took a shit. At the top of his voice he shouted, 'STAND BY YOUR BEDS.'

I was the last one out of my bunk. Quickly, I smoothed the covers flat and plumped my pillow, but it hadn't gone unnoticed. The Sergeant had clocked me out of the corner of his eye. He tapped his baton on the side of his leg as he did his early morning inspection. One by one he walked in front of us. When he got to me he stopped, pushed his baton under my pillow and flicked it on the ground. I was annoyed and held my breath. He opened my locker and emptied its entire contents on the floor. My belongings rolled under the bed. I felt my heart start to pound. Fucking liberty, I thought, but managed to stay calm. On the outside I was cool, but inside I was a seething volcano ready to erupt at any moment. I just wanted the Sergeant to go away and leave me alone. Instead, he stood in front of me, the tip of his nose touching mine, his eyes gazed unblinkingly. He pointed to the floor at my scattered belongings.

'Pick them up,' he hissed.

That was it, he'd pushed his luck too far. I felt the adrenalin rush. It flared up inside me, starting from my feet, and surged throughout my body making me feel ten times stronger. There was a banging in my head but this was no headache, it was an anger so raw, so uncontrollable, it erupted in violence. I knew what was coming, but the Sergeant didn't until he hit the ground. The other soldiers were stunned. One asked, 'Fuck me, Roy, where did you learn to punch like that?'

I laughed. 'It's either learn to punch or eat shit and I don't like to eat shit.'

Before I knew it, I was handcuffed and escorted by two Regimental Policemen to Colchester Army Prison. I had been sentenced to nine months in the Glass House.

Colchester was brutal. From the minute I stepped foot in the reception, I was confronted by tough, unrelenting, abusive Staff Sergents. They were absolute bastards. The first thing that struck me was their appearance. Everything about them was immaculate, from their peak caps shielding their vindinctive eyes to the shiny buckles on their belts. Everything at Colchester was done at the double, everything had to be quick, quick, quick.

I was marched into the reception at the double, 'Left, right ... left, right.' I had no time to think. A Sergeant barked at me, 'From now on you call me Staff, not Sir.'

Two more bastards stood either side of me bellowing in my ear in stereo, 'You got that, Shaw? ... Staff, not Sir. You got that?'

How dare they talk to me like that? I wasn't a fucking kid.

In that split second all my pent-up fury at the Army exploded out of me. There was no way some army slag was going to take liberties with me, or humiliate me in public.

'YEAH,' I shouted. 'I GOT IT. Now you get this.' I whacked the closest Staff Sergeant and leaned down and bellowed in his face, 'Now you call me Mister Shaw. You got that?'

The remaining Sergeants jumped on me and manhandled me across a courtyard to what was known as the 'singles'. It was a brick building, 200 yards away from the rest of the camp and away from the other soldiers. In the singles you were completely alone at the mercy of the Staff Sergeants. They dragged me into a cell and set about me one by one. It was in my nature to fight back and I gave them a run for their money, but there were too many of them. After the beating, I was left in the freezing brick out-house all night. I huddled in the corner trying to keep warm. My body ached from the bashing I'd received. The wind howled through the gaps under the door and through the feeding hole in the wall. It was a long night.

At first light, the cell door was flung open.

'Get up, Shaw, on the double.'

I was ordered to strip naked and was marched into a small yard. Four officers were waiting. One of them turned a heavy-duty hosepipe on me. The freezing water stung my body, the force knocking me backwards. I tried to shield myself from the drenching. I could barely catch my breath. Eventually, they turned the hose off and I slumped to the ground, gasping for air.

The Staff Sergeants laughed. I was bruised, battered and drenched but still I wouldn't give in. I rushed at the dirty bastard holding the hose and we fell to the ground. I was butt-naked, but we kicked and gouged each other in a pool of icy cold water.

Again, I was overpowered and locked back in the cell. I yelled at them, 'I'LL NEVER GIVE IN. NEVER.'

It was a battle of wills. They must have sensed my determination because after seven days of being drenched and fighting tooth and nail, I was allowed back with the mainstream prisoners.

Back in the main prison I was put into a unit with 14 other prisoners, where all of us were half-starved. Our food was weighed out and rationed, and each potato, each sausage was just enough to keep us alive.

After our pittance of a meal, we were allowed to sit in the old Nissan hut for a chat and a smoke, with each man being given one cigarette. Before we were allowed to leave, the cigarette butts were collected and counted. It was just another futile rule to break us. It didn't matter a fuck to me – I didn't smoke. While in the Nissan hut, I got chatting to another prisoner who told me about the boxing matches that were held against each unit. Boxing – that was just the job, just what I needed, somewhere to channel my aggression. It had been building up because of the consistent routine, routine and then more routine, and also because of the brutality we all suffered from the authorities. At first, I fought back out of principle but the Staff Sergeants were ruthless bastards. Slowly, that principle turned into survival.

The boxing matches were held monthly between each unit. The challenge was open to anyone who thought they were good enough to compete. And that was everybody because everyone in Colchester had been kicked out of their regiment and were there for some misdemeanour or other. The men were tough nuts from all over the country who wouldn't bow to authority, and would have been in prison if they hadn't been in the Army. They all thought they were tough, but to me they were pussy cats.

My first opponent was Big Jock, a Glaswegian with natural strength and ruggedness. All the men had been talking about him and his tremendous one-punch hitting power, especially with his right fist. I was quietly confident as I climbed into the ring. I wasn't frightened of anyone, least of all a 'sweaty sock' from north of the border. In the first round I floored him with a right hook, and caught my elbow in his nose splitting it as cleanly as if I had hit him with a hatchet.

My next fight was with a big heavily tattooed Liverpudlian from Unit C. He had fought everyone and had knocked them all out. He swaggered into the ring and I looked at his hairy shoulders as he blew the snot from his nose on to the canvas. I thought to myself that Liverpudlians had no class. The bell rang. He rushed at me, I clipped him with a left hook and followed with a right. He swayed back and forth looking like a cartoon character, then over he went.

Once the Liverpudlian hit the canvas, I earned instant respect not only from the men but particularly from the Staff Sergeant who was organising the boxing. He took a shine to me and wanted to look after his protégé. I became his star.

I was kept at Colchester Army Prison for nine months. Boxing kept me out of trouble, and it offered me a way of releasing my aggression and doing the thing I loved best – fighting. At the end of my sentence, I was posted to Hurford in Germany.

We travelled to Germany on a cargo ship. The crossing was rough and I was seasick, most of the men were. It was the first time I'd been abroad and it had to be Germany. The war had only been over for nine years and there was still an underlying resentment. The Germans didn't like us and the feeling was mutual. It was too soon to forgive and forget the atrocities of the war, the memories of lost loved ones were still prominent in our minds and wounds hadn't had time to heal.

In Germany, my first military manoeuvre was to be a raid by Dutch soldiers. It was only an exercise, not a real raid. I was part of a convoy of lorries, but my vehicle was pulled out because it was the Signals truck. I was ordered to park a fair distance from the rest and stay on look-out duty. I parked the lorry in a secluded part of the woods. I was feeling knackered so I lay down on the long bench seat and fell fast asleep.

Suddenly, I was woken by a terrific noise. It was like New Year's Eve and Guy Fawkes night all rolled into one. I fell out of my lorry still half asleep and scared to death. The sound of bangers and fire-crackers going off was all around me, and in my dazed state I thought, Fuck me, it's for real – I'm being attacked.

I dived into a ditch flat on my belly and edged my way through the mud on my elbows, just how the Army had taught me. My only thought was to get back to my regiment. The noise of bombs exploding and guns firing was deafening, it was complete mayhem everywhere. I crawled through a hedgerow and, to my horror, came face to face with the enemy – six Dutch soldiers. Instinctively I pulled out my rifle and smashed one in the face with the butt of my gun. He went down. Then I swung round and took out a second. A third jumped me from behind. I flung him over my shoulder on to the ground and sank the butt of the rifle into his chest. He gave out a gasp. Another Dutch soldier put his hands up in defeat and walked backwards shouting, 'NO ... NO.' But I'd lost all sense of reality. I thought they were real soldiers and this was a real war, and I was fighting it alone.

The Dutchman must have seen the dangerous gleam in my eyes and the flash of my gun. He turned on his heels and fled, and I fired my rifle into the darkness indiscriminately! My only thought then was to get back to my regiment. I bolted back, eager to report the incident. I was breathless as I rushed into camp.

'In the woods ...' I gasped, 'soldiers ... I, er ... I, er ...'

Halfway through my sentence, four Dutch soldiers limped into the camp, two with broken noses, and one doubled up clutching his chest unable to breath properly. My unit was none too pleased, and neither was the CO. I was confined to barracks pending a court martial.

Being on open arrest, unable to leave the barracks, soon pissed me off. All the other men were going out one evening to a local German dance hall and casino called The Gorilla Club. It had been arranged for weeks, and everybody had been looking forward to cutting loose for the night. I sat on my bunk and watched them all getting ready. I listened to them talking about how drunk they were going to get and how many German birds they were going to pull. I was gutted, everyone was going except me. I decided I couldn't and wouldn't be left out. I was going and to hell with the consequences.

I made arrangements with my old mate Jimmy Baggott. Jimmy was a tall, blue-eyed blond and extremely good looking – in fact, he looked more German than a German. We arranged to meet later at the dance hall. I waited until all the men had gone and I had the barracks to myself apart from the guards. I waited patiently until it got dark, then managed to slip out through the window in the latrines and made my way to the dance hall. Jimmy was waiting, he was already half-pissed. We leant on the bar, ordered a round of beers, started drinking and scanned the room for birds. It was good to feel normal again, if only for a while.

We were having a whale of a time, laughing and joking, when two German girls at a nearby table gave us the eye. One was a beautiful buxom blonde, the other was enormous and looked like she could pack a punch. We sent them over a drink. Jimmy winked and said, 'Fuck me, Roy, we're in here, but I don't fancy yours much.'

Jimmy walked over and asked the blonde to dance. In broken English, she mumbled something about a list. He couldn't understand what she meant and told her to forget all about the list and to dance with him. He took her hand and pulled her towards the dance floor. She yanked her arm back and started shouting. Jimmy looked back at me and shrugged his shoulders. The two girls jumped up from the table, the big one rolling up her sleeves ready for a punch-up. I started to laugh. Sensing trouble, the doormen from the Casino came over; they were the biggest doormen I have ever seen. They tried to calm the situation by explaining we had to put our name on a list for a dance with the girls and to wait our turn. Jimmy told the doormen to fuck off. I didn't want any trouble – I shouldn't have been there in the first place, and trouble was the last thing I needed. I told Jimmy to leave it out, but he was having none of it. He held up a bottle and hissed, 'Do you want it, you kraut bastard?'

I closed my eyes, flinched, and thought, that's torn it. The big doorman drew his lips back in a half smile that resembled a snarl. I knew then it was going to go off. I whispered to Jimmy out of the corner of my mouth, 'I'll take the biggest one.'

The doorman stepped forward, resembling a giant oak tree as he stood in front of me. I looked him up and down, from his snarl to his clenched fists. His arms were so bowed he looked like he was holding two rolled-up carpets under them.

I thought, Oh fuck, how the hell am I going to knock him over? He was a gorilla in every sense of the word, particularly as he worked at The Gorilla Club. I weighed up the situation, and knew if I just threw a punch it would lose power by the time it hit him because of his height. I'd have to throw my whole weight behind it. I clenched my fist, drew back and twisted from my waist. I hit him with a left hook followed by a right uppercut. He wobbled, then wobbled again, and over he went like a big ol' tree.

Jimmy and I looked at each other.

'Let's get the fuck out of here.'

We started to run before the doorman got up. The crowded dance floor parted like the Red Sea to let us through. As we reached the double doors to the hall, Jim pushed one door and ran through. I pushed the other but my side was locked and I went through the stained-glass window and cut my hand badly. We ran around the narrow streets trying to get away from the area until we found a quiet, seedy bar on the outskirts of town. We went in and sat in the corner, trying to look inconspicuous. Twenty minutes later, the police arrived.

'Any Englishmen must make themselves known.'

The landlord pointed to us. I tried to hide my cut hand under the table to avoid drawing attention to us, but the policeman noticed it.

'Vot have you done to your hand?' he asked.

I told him I was a mechanic and had cut my hand at work. He didn't believe me and ordered us outside. As we walked towards the door, I whispered to Jimmy, 'When we get outside, have it away on your toes.'

As we went through the doors, we started to run as fast as we could, but found it difficult because we had been drinking too much. It felt like holding a barrel of beer, only it was in my belly. We were puffing and panting, with the police hot on our tails.

'Stop, or I'll shoot, English bastards.'

Jimmy and I kept on going, not daring to look round. A bullet whizzed past our heads. It only made us run faster. Jimmy ran so fast I thought he was hanging on to the bullet. He ran one way, I ran the other, and I never saw Jimmy's arse again for dust. I continued up a hill, but I was exhausted. The German police meant business and shouted, 'STOP, OR I'LL SHOOT.'

I thought, fucking cheek, we won the war. What am I running for? I put my hands up in the air signalling defeat. The police surrounded me, pointing their guns at my head saying, 'You come with us.'

I didn't argue with them. I wasn't daft and, besides, I was knackered. They took me to the local police station and I was nicked. I was taken back to the barracks and put under close arrest. Yet another court martial.

The next morning, I was marched by two Regimental Policemen in to see the Commanding Officer.

'Left, right ... left, right. Stop. Face your Commanding Officer.'

The CO didn't give me a chance to say a word.

'Shaw,' he said, 'you're the scum of the earth.'

Scum of the earth! Who the fuck did he think he was talking to? What a liberty. I didn't say a word. I jumped over the table and head-butted him. The Regimental Policemen grabbed me. They were tough bastards but I put up a good fight. There was blood and teeth everywhere. Obviously, I was overpowered and slung into a cell. Later, one of the RPs came back to see me. I thought we were going to have a row, but instead he took time out and explained that he recognised himself in me, that he also used to be anti-authority, and said I wasn't doing myself any favours. If I continued, he said, I'd be going away for a long time. He made it clear the only way I had any chance of getting out of three court martials was to see the doctor and tell him I was hearing voices.

'Hearing voices!' I laughed. 'Are you sure?'

The next morning, I was in the doctor's office. He asked me if I had anything to say. I shook my head.

On the way out, the RP asked me if I'd told the doctor about the voices. I told him I hadn't. He went back into the office and returned a few minutes later with the doctor. It had given me enough time to think about it.

'Tell the doctor what you told me, Roy, about the voices. You know ... the ones in your head.'

On the spur of the moment I had to make up a story, something I would remember. I told him that I heard voices, one a woman called Jean and the other one called John. John would tell me to hurt people and Jean would tell me not to. I explained that I felt I was torn between good and evil.

'Ahh,' the German doctor said, 'you crazy.'

The RP stood behind the doctor, stuck his thumb in the air and winked. I didn't know what he was looking so pleased about. I was taken directly to a German mental asylum. My feet didn't touch the ground. I was taken to the nut house so quickly it made my head spin.

Nobody spoke as I was marched into the asylum. The RPs handed me over to the psychiatrist who was sitting behind a large desk with a strange little smile on his face. I spat my gum on to the floor and looked around at the high ceilings and barred windows. I wasn't bothered, I thought I could bluff my way through; being there was just a means to an end.

A doctor and two male nurses led me down a long corridor, on each side of which were heavy steel doors that were bolted. I was taken into a ward with rows of beds on each side, each one containing a patient with a vacant look in their eyes. I was shown to a bed at the end of the ward and told to get undressed.

Over the next few days, I was seen by an endless stream of doctors and nurses. No one spoke proper English, so I could barely understand what they were saying. I just nodded and agreed and made the right noises at the right times, or so I thought.

After much prodding and poking it was decided that the best way to treat me was with electrical stimulation to the brain.

'What the fuck is electrical-what's-its-name to the brain?' I asked.

The nurses tutted, sighed and dismissed the question with a wave of the hand.

The next morning, I was taken to a ward containing seven men lying on either side of the room. All were tucked up in bed, crisp white sheets pulled tightly across their shoulders, their heads being the only thing exposed. I sat on my bed looking at these poor souls, they were like the living dead. Four male nurses motioned to me to go with them. I went voluntarily. A doctor patted a leather table for me to lie on. Everyone was chatting and didn't seem to care about me; it was all in a day's work to them. I looked around the room at the medical equipment, the big dials and volt meters. Lying next to the leather table was an instrument that looked like a stethoscope.

Anxiously, I climbed onto the table. The doctor pulled me backwards and four men, two either side, held my legs. I started to get a bit nervous and asked them what they were doing. They smiled like smiling vipers. Two more nurses held my arms, then another pushed a large brown rubber object into my mouth which made me gag.

I couldn't move and started to panic. My heart was pounding. Someone wet my temples. Suddenly I felt a searing pain in my head. It felt as though my brain was frying. My body tightened. Then nothing ...

I woke up in a white room with a crisp white sheet tight across my shoulders. At first, I was puzzled. I didn't know where I was. I looked at the strangers lying in the beds either side of me. I felt strange. Peaceful. Calm. I had never felt like that before. It was then I realised I had become one of those poor souls with the vacant look in their eyes.

Slowly, my memory started flooding back. That room. The equipment. Those dials. A nurse told me I had been given ECT (electroconvulsive therapy) and that I was going to have eight sessions of it.

A few days later, a nurse came back to take me for the second ECT, and this time I was a bit more wary. When I walked into the treatment room there were more male nurses than before. I discovered later that when I'd had my first ECT I convulsed so badly and lashed out so much that I hurt a few of the male nurses who'd been holding me down. This time they were taking no chances. There were four nurses holding my legs on each side and four holding my arms. Just in case.

After my eight treatments of ECT, the German doctor came to see me and explained that my brain cells had been muddled up – effectively, the electric shock treatment had exploded them. When the cells had settled back down, they were supposed to heal in basically the right place. He said that ECT was vital for my recovery. I thought what a load of bollocks it all was, and that the imaginary Jean and John had a lot to answer for.

I stayed at the German asylum for six weeks, after which I was shipped back to England to an army institution called Netley in Southampton. I remained at Netley until I was given a dishonourable discharge for being mad. That was the first time I came face to face with insanity. But it certainly wasn't to be my last.

CHAPTER 3

SHORT, SHARP, SHOCK

'For a while we were riding high, but we were total amateurs, and never even tried to lie low. One minute I was working on a building site and potless – next I'm Jack the Lad, flashing the cash. But the police aren't always daft ...'

I T WAS GOOD TO BE BACK HOME IN ENGLAND living with my mum after my disastrous experiences in the Army. I landed a job on a building site in Ilford, Essex, as a hod-carrier, which meant I had to race up and down a ladder all day supplying bricks and mortar to the brickies. It was back-breaking work for little money. I'd get home every night, filthy dirty, knackered, I was earning peanuts and was pissed off.

I got in late one night and, as usual, Mum was in the kitchen. I took my boots off by the back door and called out to her, 'What's for dinner, Mum?'

'Steak and kidney pudding, but it's probably dried up by now,' she said with some irritation.

I washed my hands under the tap, kissed her on the cheek and said, 'Ooh, steak and kidney pudding, my favourite.'

All I was interested in was eating my grub – after a rotten day at work, a piping hot dinner was my saving grace. I looked forward to it each evening until, that is, my sister's boyfriend, Terry the teddy boy, walked in. He was a flash git and always wore nice suits with velvet collars, and never seemed to get dirty, unlike me. I often wondered how he could afford those suits; he never had a regular job, but always had plenty of money.

Terry stood in the middle of the front room preening himself in front of a guitar-shaped mirror that hung above the fireplace. He swept his greasy hair back into a 'DA' while whistling a Lonny Donegan tune. I glanced up and looked him up and down. He was wearing a new suit, electric blue with a navy blue velvet collar, and I wanted one.

'Where did you get that suit?' I asked.

He winked, clicked his tongue, and with a wry smile said, 'Do you want a suit like mine, Roy? I know just how you can get one.'

I pushed aside my half-eaten dinner and said, 'I'm all ears.'

He told me about a robbery he was planning. Suddenly, the penny dropped. Terry was a 'tea-leaf' – a robber. That's how he made his money and that's how he could afford his flash suits. The cunning bastard.

Terry explained that a bookie he knew had been evading the tax man by syphoning off huge amounts of money and he kept the cash at his house in Southend.

'Roy, it's there for the taking. Easy money.'

I didn't hesitate. 'Count me in.'

Terry had inside information and knew the day when the bookie took the money to his house in Southend. We took another mate with us called Eric, and waited outside the bookie's shop until the bloke came out and got into his car, hopefully with the money. We followed him all the way to Southend, keeping well back but never letting him out of our sight for a moment. We watched him pull his Jaguar on to his drive, and with one final drag on his big cigar, he leaned over the back seat and grabbed a holdall.

Terry nudged me, 'That's where he keeps the money – in the holdall.'

We waited until the bookie had gone inside, then knocked on the door and stood waiting for it to open. Looking back on it now, we were complete amateurs, we'd made no preparations, we had no balaclavas, no gloves, nothing. It seemed to take an eternity for the door to open but in reality it must have only been minutes.

We stood waiting on the doorstep, our heads tucked down against the icy drizzle, anxiously fidgeting and saying quietly to ourselves, 'Come on, come on.'

The door opened slightly, and instinctively we barged in. Terry grabbed the bookie round the waist, I put my hand over his mouth from behind, and Eric closed the door. Hearing the scuffle, his wife came out of the kitchen wiping her hands.

'What's going on, George? Who are all these men?'

We hadn't bargained on a woman being in the house; we hadn't given it any thought. I tried not to frighten her, and told her we'd just come to see her husband on some business – not to worry, no one would get hurt.

She stood frozen to the spot, her young son gripping her hand. I dragged the bookie into the lounge. He pleaded with me not to hurt his wife and son. I had no intention of hurting either. I would never hurt a woman or a child – I'm not an animal! So I told Eric to take the petrified woman and her son into another room, out of the way.

I tied the bookie to a chair and asked him politely where the money was. He shook his head in denial. 'What money?'

I slapped him hard across the face. 'I won't ask you again. Where's the fucking money?'

'What money, there ain't no money,' he lied.

I was having none of it.

'Look,' I said, 'either way I'm walking out of here with that money. You can either give it to me the easy way or the hard way. You choose. Tell me where the money is, or I'll make you. It's up to you.'

Just to help him think, I gave him a jab, his head jerked backwards and a small trickle of blood dribbled from his nose. Still he refused to tell me. I was livid and set about him.

Bang. 'Where's the money?' Bang. 'Where's the money?' Bang.

'It's in the back of the cabinet in a biscuit tin,' he screamed out in defeat.

We grabbed the huge tin, that was the only thing on our minds. We never dared to look inside; for all we knew it could have been full of biscuits. But it wasn't – it was full of money, lots and lots of money. Back home, we emptied the tin on to the blue Formica-topped table in the kitchen, looked at each other, rubbed our hands together and howled with laughter. Eagerly, the money was counted – there was £3,000. We thought we'd hit the jackpot. It was carved up three ways – a grand apiece. That was a lot of money in 1955, near enough the price of a small house.

I told Mum to give up work. I said I had done a lot of overtime and I could afford it, and she believed me! I treated my sisters to the latest record player, but best of all I was now the flash git in the fine suits and crocodile shoes.

For a while we were riding high, but we were total amateurs, and never even tried to lie low. One minute I was working on a building site and potless – next I'm Jack the Lad, flashing the cash. The police ain't daft, and they soon arrested me and I was charged with robbery. I was sentenced to Borstal; the Judge said I needed a short, sharp shock.

He specified a sentence, and said if I behaved I'd do nine months. If not, I'd do three years. I didn't give a fuck – I could do nine months or three years. My motto is, if you can't do the time, don't commit the crime.

I was put on a coach with eight other cons, all of us having been sentenced to a Borstal. The dim ones went to Feltham in Middlesex, and the more uncontrollable were taken to the secure Borstal at Usk in Wales.

The journey to Wales was a long one. I saw plenty of sheep on the way but not much else. I arrived at the Borstal around midday. It was divided up into two sections, one being the Camp, and the other, the Jug. The day I arrived there happened to be a boxing match between the Camp and the Jug. I couldn't believe my luck. I told one of the screws that I had done some boxing in the Army.

'Oh, 'ave ya?' he said. 'Let's see what you can do now ...'

He put me into spar with the toughest boy of the Camp, who was known as the 'daddy', but two murderous left hooks and he was down. Then the screws brought in the 'daddy' of the Jug. He laughed and said, 'You can have it with me now.'

I didn't bother sparring with him either. I attacked him with cold, controlled ferocity, knocking him spark out. I raised my arms in victory because I was the 'daddy' of both camps now.

Although the 'daddies' had a reputation for being bullies, I had no intention of becoming a bully myself. A look from me was enough to get what I wanted, and being a 'daddy' had certain advantages, like other inmates making me a cup of tea and generally being at my beck and call.

I was not only the 'daddy' of the Borstal, but I was doing the Governor a favour by keeping order. There was no fighting, no bullying, I wouldn't allow it. If there was anything or anyone to take care of, I would be the one to do it. The Governor recognised my capabilities and the unofficial power I had. He knew it was in his best interests to keep me sweet – well, after all, I was practically doing his job.

I was allocated some work outside the Borstal cutting down trees in the nearby forest. The man in charge of the works detail was a tough bastard, with hands like shovels. He was a typical forester, all tartan shirts and chain-saw. He thought all the boys from the Borstal were no-good toe-rags and took great delight in working them 'til they dropped. Well, I knew his little game and I also knew what he was up to. The other boys might have been lazy little tykes but not me – the harder I worked, the harder Chain-Saw Charlie pushed, and the harder Chain-Saw Charlie pushed, the harder I worked.

Old Charlie may well have been chopping down trees for forty years or more, and I may well have been a jumped-up little cockney, but he couldn't deny that I was able to keep up with him tree for tree, and within a week we became friends – he even gave me one of his tartan shirts!

All in all, I had things pretty much under control at the

Borstal. I had a good job, my little yes-men running errands, extra visits from my mum and the Govenor, more or less, in my pocket. Life for me was relatively simple, until, that is, I met Flapper Stern and Roy Buckley. The new boys.

They were flash, street-wise tough nuts, and I liked them instantly. Flapper, as he was known because of the size of his ears, was a 'wannabe' gangster. He had all the mannerisms of the movie star James Cagney, who always played gangsters in the black-and-white films. Flapper held his elbows to his side as if he was holding his trousers up and spoke through gritted teeth, calling everyone 'You dirty rat' and said 'Yeah' after everything he said.

'I'm making a break for it, yeah ... I'm heading for the bright lights of London and the dirty rats will never find us, yeah ... There's plenty of booze, birds and fast cars, yeah. They won't never find me there, yeah ... Come wiv us, Roy. Yeah ... come wiv us ...'

He kept on and on and made escaping sound so good that eventually I agreed to go with them and on the spur of the moment I said, 'Count me in. Yeah. . . I'll 'ave some of that. Yeah. . . ' It was frightening – I was even starting to sound like Flapper.

The plan was for us to escape in the Borstal doctor's car. For a week we watched the doctor's movements, clocking him park his car in the same spot at the rear of his surgery. Every Monday he held a night-time surgery, and the following Monday we made ready for our escape. Flapper, Buckley and I waited until surgery was finished, then sneaked out of our dormitory. We hid behind the doctor's green Morris Minor and waited for him to come out. His keys jangled as he locked his surgery for the night. We kept as quiet and as still as we could.

'I'll do 'im,' I said, 'I'll bash 'im over the head.'

'Yeah ... That's it, do the dirty rat,' growled Flapper.

Flapper was beginning to irritate me – there's only so much James Cagney a man can take. I gave him a sideways glance and tutted. Fucking James Cagney. I didn't know whether to hit him or the fucking doctor. There is a time and a place to muck about but not when you are about to cave someone's skull in. The doctor fumbled to unlock his car. I started to feel anxious, my heart was pounding and my mouth felt dry. I clenched my fist so tight it turned my knuckles white.

The doctor dropped his car keys on the ground, bent down to pick them up, and as he stood up I punched him in the back of his head. He fell as if he had been filleted, his body slithering down the car. Quickly, we grabbed him and dragged him behind the dustbins. I jumped into the driver's seat, rammed the car into gear, and sped out of the Borstal heading towards London.

Now, I didn't realise that driving a Morris Minor would be quite so different from driving the three-ton lorry I was used to. I pushed, pulled and crunched the gears. Flapper leaned over the front seat and said, 'Roy, it's a gearbox, not a fucking juke box.'

'Shut up, Cagney, I'm driving.'

By the time we reached Oxford, the car ran out of petrol. It was Buckley's bright idea to get away from the main road and find a railway station. It was midnight and a light rain began to fall as we made our way across the open fields. Soon we became caked in mud, and could barely lift our feet. We ran through the brambles and through the bushes, through ditches and over fences until we reached a railway crossing.

We clambered aboard an open coal train, hoping it was going in the right direction. By the time we jumped off we were as black as coal. I looked at Flapper; he no longer looked like James Cagney, more like Al Jolson.

When we finally reached London we decided to split up and go our separate ways and, to be honest, I had had just about enough of their company. They'd made escaping sound so good, but it wasn't all it was cracked up to be. Now I had to find somewhere safe to stay and with someone I trusted. I thought of Uncle Bert, my dad's brother, whom I'd always got on well with. I made my way to their house in Christian Street, Stepney.

Aunty Ivy opened the door and laughed. 'What on earth's happened to you, Roy?'

I explained I was on the run from Borstal. I must have

looked a right sight – I was cold, hungry and dirty. Aunt Ivy ran me a hot bath. I huddled round the fire in the front room while Bert made me a door-stop cheese sandwich. 'Don't worry, boy, we'll get you sorted.'

By tea time the next day, Bert had got me a job in a chair factory, off the Commercial Road, East London. My job was working on the pullies hauling up the chairs. It was great because it made my arms strong. I worked all day at the chair factory, and went to a local gym at night for my boxing. I settled down into this twilight world of make believe under the false name of Roy West, a name I'd plucked from nowhere, but if I'd known then what I know now, I would never have chosen the name because of the infamous mass murderer, Fred West.

Although I had a job, boxing was my whole life – I ate, drank and slept boxing. That was all Bert and I talked about, and he took a great interest in my training. He even came to watch me spar, and after knocking someone out one night he was surprised how good I had become. He promised he would introduce me to a boxing promotor he knew, by the name of Mickey Praeger. Praeger owned a duffle coat factory near Spitalfield market.

Uncle Bert was as good as his word and the following week we went to meet him. We stood in the pub waiting for Mickey to arrive. He walked in, saw Uncle Bert and, with an outstretched hand, approached us.

'Mickey,' said Uncle Bert, 'glad you could make it. Thanks for coming. Let me introduce you to my boy, Roy West.'

I looked at Mickey's face. It seemed familiar, and while someone else in the bar caught his attention, I whispered to Bert, 'I've seen him somewhere before.' But the name, Mickey Praeger, didn't ring any bells. Bert replied, 'It's Mickey Duff, you doughnut. His real name is Praeger but he changed his name to Duff because of the duffle coat factory his family owned.'

I laughed to myself to think that if the world-famous Mickey Duff owned an anorak factory, he could have ended up as Mickey Anorak.

Later that evening, Mickey took me to his gym in Great

Portland Street to see how I shaped up. I sensed that Duff probably thought I was just another delinquent kid looking for salvation in the ring, like so many before and since, and I was only there on the say-so of my uncle. Duff wasn't taking too much notice of me. Was he just going through the motions or was it a favour he owed my uncle? We walked into his gym, where the smell of sweat and leather was overwhelming. Mickey sat ringside and told a fighter to get ready.

I changed into my shorts and boots, pulled on my gloves and stood in the corner of the ring. My first opponent was a slugger with a corrogated nose. He was so obviously a fighter whose job it was to sort out the men from the boys. I put my hands up to guard my face and went at him. I hit him with a left hook, followed by a right uppercut and in those two punches the damage was done. He fell to his knees. I turned my head and looked at Duff – now I had his attention.

'Just a fluke,' he said.

I was confident and asked, 'Who's next?'

The ref held the ropes apart and in came number two.

'Work him,' shouted Duff.

The first round was even. He hit me with a few good body blows, but early in the second he missed with a right and started to throw a left, but I side-stepped it and with a classic short right, he went down. I looked at Bert, who was grinning from ear to ear. I almost heard him say to Duff, 'I told you so.'

There and then Duff took me on, and I signed a contract. He explained I wouldn't be earning much money in the beginning, but he was prepared to wait until I earned big money, then he would take his cut.

I changed gyms and started training at the famous Thomas a'Beckett in the Old Kent Road. I had a new trainer, too – Danny Holland. The best. Also training at the gym were Terry Spinks (who went on to win a gold medal at the Olympics) and Terry Downs, the irrepressible cockney character from Paddington in West London, who later brought the World Middleweight title back to Britain.

A lot of good boxers came out of the Thomas a'Beckett. I learnt a lot from the professionals, but two guys I never got to spar with, because they were heavyweights, were twins Henry and George Cooper. I used to watch Henry Cooper sparring to see how he ducked away from punches. He was a true professional, a great boxer.

By day I worked at the chair factory and at night I trained at the gym. On the way home after training one night, I stopped off for a drink in The Artichoke pub in Stepney Way, with a couple of mates – Albert Rainbird and big Lennie Ketley. Albert later turned out to be a grass, one I eventually sorted out, but I'll explain and go into gory detail later.

We entered the crowded pub, and made our way through to the bar and ordered our drinks. Standing beside us was a gigantic man sizing us up. I didn't recognise him but I had a gut feeling he wanted to say something.

'What are you boys doing in here?' the big fella asked. 'Got a couple of brasses?'

'No. Not at all. I was thirsty and I wanted a drink,' I answered. I thought it was a bit of a cheek and took an instant dislike to him, but didn't say anything because I thought Rainbird knew him. When the big fella walked away, I asked Albert if he knew him. He said he didn't know him personally but had heard of his reputation. His name was Big Jacko. I didn't give a fuck about his reputation or how big he was; how dare he ask me if I was there for the brasses, what business was it of his? Albert told me to say nothing but I was annoyed. I followed Big Jacko into the toilet and pulled him.

'What's it got to do with you what I'm doing, and where I'm going?'

Albert walked in holding a smashed bottle. Big Jacko smirked.

'So, you boys wanna play wiv bottles do ya?'

I turned to Albert and told him to fuck off and said to Jacko, 'No, just you and me outside.'

When we got outside the pub, Jacko put his right hand in his back pocket. I thought he was going to pull a knife so I kicked him hard in the nuts and with a right hook square on the chin, over he went, he didn't know what had hit him. Albert appeared from nowhere and went to kick him. I put my arm up to stop him. Once I do a bloke, I do him, I don't need any help. Jacko was down and out for the count and as far as I was concerned that was that. I walked away. As we were walking back to the car, a crowd of people came out of the pub and helped Jacko to his feet. One of them said, 'It took six of them to bash Jacko.' I was incensed. Fucking liberty.

'Six of 'em?' I snarled. 'I done him by myself.'

The crowd obviously didn't believe me. I walked back to Jacko and grabbed him by the collar and said, 'Tell 'em, Roy Shaw done you by himself.'

He said nothing, just spat blood from his mouth.

'I said, tell 'em, Shawy done you by himself.'

He mumbled the words, 'Shawy done me by himself.'

I shook him and screamed, 'louder.'

Again he mumbled, 'Shawy done me by himself.'

I shook him again. 'Louder.'

At the top of his voice he shouted, 'Shawy done me by himself.'

Just for good measure I whacked him again, and over he went.

'See,' I reminded the crowd, 'by myself.'

The following Friday you could have heard a pin drop as I walked into The Artichoke alone, and ordered a drink. If Big Jacko or his family wanted to make a mountain out of a molehill and do anything about the fight, then this was their chance. I looked around, but there was no sign of Big Jacko or his family.

A man approached me and introduced himself as Sam McCarthy, a lightweight boxer. He'd witnessed the rise and the fall of the big fella the previous week and said he could arrange a manager for me. I declined, and said I was with Mickey Duff.

I had my first professional fight for Duff at Wembley Town hall against a kid called Denis Wingrove from Dagenham. Duff said my first fight would be an easy one, so when he told me my opponent was Denis Wingrove I said, 'An easy fight? You've got to be fucking joking.'

Denis and Roy Wingrove were two brothers who came from my manor. Denis was the biggest of the two and the toughest. He was a big, stocky, well-built lad with ginger hair, and a red-hot temper to match. I had seen him have a couple of rows and I knew he was a right handful. He was a colourful and charismatic figure with the potential to become one of the best and Duff said he was easy.

I laughed and said, 'If you consider Denis Wingrove an easy fight, I don't know what your hard fights are going to be like.'

Wembley Town Hall was packed to the rafters, the fight was a sell-out. Mickey had promoted the fight well, and everyone had come to see the new youngsters slug it out. For an hour before the fight I sat in my dressing room. I could feel the tension winding up in the hall like a tight coiled spring, fuelled by lager and bravado.

At 8.00pm when the lights went down, it was as if someone had hit the pause button and the hall was plunged into momentary darkness. The hall held its collective breath as the MC climbed into the ring in his dinner suit. His outsize bow-tie was like a propeller. He wore a red ruffled shirt and cuban-heeled boots, and pranced around the ring like a chicken shaking its tail feathers.

'Ladies and Gentlemen, introducing in the red corner for his first début as a professional boxer, fighting out of Stepney, East London ... Rrrrrrrrrrrroy West.'

The crowd jumped to their feet, clapping and whistling. I acknowledged them by bowing my head.

'And in the blue corner, fighting out of Dagenham, Essex ... Denis Winnnnnngrove.'

The house lights faded, and you could smell the violence in the air.

Denis removed his silk gown and limbered up. I had no need for such flamboyance. I just wore plain black boots and black shorts. I rolled my neck from side to side to release the tension. The referee motioned us to the middle of the ring.

'Touch gloves, boys, and have a good clean fight.'

The bell rang, my nerves disappeared. Wingrove looked

excellent for three rounds, he boxed cleverly against me, stabbing out his left lead and scoring many points. Suddenly, the fight took a dramatic turn. I threw a right, and Wingrove lost his balance and fell backwards across the middle of the ropes.

For a few seconds he was stretched across the ropes completely helpless and it was touch and go whether he'd topple over backwards and fall out of the ring on to the press benches. Had this happened, Wingrove may never have climbed back in time to beat the ten-second count. Luck was on his side. After swaying backwards and forwards, he finally regained his balance. Wingrove fought back viciously, but it was a right to the head in the sixth round that finally nailed him. My punch split open his left eyebrow and soon his face was covered in blood.

The fight went the distance. It was such a good fight and I beat him fair and square. The crowd showed their appreciation by throwing money in the ring which was the done thing in those days. The money was halved between the two fighters as a show of appreciation for putting on a good fight. The next day in all the papers the headlines read: DREAM DÉBUT OF NEW FIGHTER. For that fight I received £21 for a single night's work. True to his word, Mickey Duff never took a penny from my early fights, saying that when I started to earn big money he'd take his cut. He was a good manager, and is top of the tree now. Years later, in an interview in Time Out magazine, he was quoted as saying, 'Roy Shaw was one of the most promising prospects I have ever had at that time in my career.'

At that time, I was fighting under the name of Roy West. I had to, I was still on the run from Borstal. I had ten fights with Duff in ten weeks, six ending in KOs. I was riding high and felt unstoppable until, that is, Christmas Eve 1956. My career as a professional boxer came to a dramatic end at the Ilford Palais.

I was the local celebrity standing in the Ilford Palais in my new teddy-boy suit and I felt great. While 'Jail House Rock' blared out from the record player, I jived with a pretty honey, who swung round showing the tops of her stockings. I felt fantastic, until five big lumps started to pull down the Christmas decorations. It was nothing to do with me, and even when one of the baubles hit me on the back of the head I ignored them because I didn't want any trouble and didn't want anything to spoil my night – besides, I was still on the run from Borstal. I recognised the trouble-makers, they were known as the big five from Canning Town, and had been a nuisance in a few clubs in the area.

The bouncers were having trouble with them. One of the bouncers was Billy Walker, the British Champion boxer known as the Blond Bomber. I knew Billy through boxing; he'd watched a few of my fights and knew I was pretty handy. He asked me to give the bouncers a hand and, always eager to please, I agreed. It turned into a free-for-all, chairs were broken and bottles were smashed. Someone punched me in the mouth and split my lip. The police were called and arrested all of us, and when my real name soon came out I was taken directly to Cardiff Prison, the nearest prison to the Borstal.

I was escorted into the jail, and met with the familiarity of the sounds of doors being kicked open or slammed shut, cons screaming, screws shouting and radios blaring. Above all this noise I heard an argument on the landing, and I recognised one of the voices straight away.

'You dirty Welsh rat.'

I buried my face in my hands and shook my head in disbelief. It was Flapper, alias fucking James Cagney, still at it.

He spotted me, stopped rowing, held his hand up to the face of the Taffy, shrugged his shoulders, leaned over the landing and shouted, 'Roy ... they got ya ... yeah ...'

Flapper and Buckley had been arrested soon after we'd escaped. They'd been in Cardiff Prison for the whole three months I'd been on the run. They were two cocky Londoners and right little rascals and by the time I landed on the prison doorstep the Welsh hated them. I didn't improve matters with my arrival, it only added fuel to the fire. I was Londoner number three, the third cocky bastard. Right from the word go I was fighting.

One morning, my cell door opened, and as usual I grabbed my pot ready to slop out. A screw put his arm across my cell door blocking my way.

'You're too old to be a young offender, Shaw. You're being taken to the man's wing today.'

I threw my pot, contents and all, into his face and slammed my cell door. I pushed my bed, table and chair up against it barricading myself in.

'I ain't going nowhere,' I screamed.

Later, an old screw came to my cell. He'd seen and heard it all before. 'Look at this grey hair. I never had a grey hair on my head 'til you three cockney bastards came here,' he said.

I listened to him. He sounded so fed up, he told me I wasn't doing myself any favours, either way I had to come out of my cell, and anyway I was due in court the next morning. Always ready to see sense, I came out. The next morning I stood in court, and got three years for bashing the Borstal doctor and escaping.

Normally after sentencing you have to wait two or three months to be allocated a prison but the Welsh were sick of us and within a day I was taken to Wormwood Scrubs in London, and then on to Lewes Prison which was a young man's prison in East Sussex.

I walked into reception and was confronted by a big geezer, a prisoner by the name of McCulloch. He was a bruiser, a Paddy, and was bragging about how hard he was. I stood in front of him, pulled my shirt open, and said, 'Punch me as hard as you can, Paddy.'

He laughed and, in a soft Irish lilt, said, 'If I punched you in the stomach, boy, my hand would go right through to your backbone.' Then he walked away. He just laughed at me. I felt stupid and humiliated. From then on, I had the instant needle with him, and whenever we met on the landing the hair on the back of my neck used to stand up, but he never confronted me. He always ignored me, which was possibly the worst thing he could have done. It was inevitable we would come to blows.

On one particular occasion, I was in the gym playing basket

ball with the other prisoners, and McCulloch was on the other team. He was built like an ox and used his size and weight to smash my team-mates to the ground at every opportunity. I got the ball. McCulloch rushed at me. I stopped dead in my tracks.

'Touch me and I'll kill ya,' I spat at him.

McCulloch's eyes narrowed and he smirked at me.

'What's the fucking matter with you?' he asked.

Suddenly I hit him under the jaw, catching him completely by surprise and flooring him, then stepped over his body and walked away.

Later that day I was called in front of the Governor. I had hurt McCulloch badly; he was in the prison hospital nursing a broken jaw.

I stood in the Governor's office while he scanned my prison record. The Guvernor shook his head.

'Shaw,' he said, 'you have got quite a reputation and up until now you have only mixed with young offenders, but now I've no hesitation in sending you to Maidstone, a man's prison – and believe me, Shaw, in Maidstone Prison it's a man's world ...'

CHAPTER 4

IT'S A MAN'S WORLD

'... somehow I fitted in with the big boys and they took to me, I felt they accepted me. I wasn't frightened of anyone, and they recognised this in me. I was one of their own – one of the chaps ...'

MAIDSTONE PRISON IS LITERALLY IN THE MIDDLE OF THE TOWN. It's an imposing solid fortress made of stone, and it's not only the prison but most of the surrounding buildings that are built of a particular type of sandstone. Maidstone is well known for its appalling one-way system – the prison acts as an island and the traffic is filtered around it. It doesn't matter where you want to go in the town, you have to drive round the prison. The traffic whizzes around the nick, the drivers oblivious to the secret life contained behind the high walls. Certain cells overlook the main road, which for the long-term prisoner makes serving their sentence difficult, witnessing life carrying on outside. Tuesday is market day in Maidstone, and the hustle and bustle of the market penetrates the cell windows and filters into the empty minds of each and every con whose only thought is his next meal.

I was handcuffed in the back of the prison van for the five-hour journey from Wales to Kent. Traffic around the prison was at a standstill because it was market day. The van eventually sped through the main gates. I got out of the van and stretched. I was a young offender entering a man's world but I was ready, and more than able, to deal with whatever lay ahead of me.

If I was looking for trouble, I had certainly come to the right place, because Maidstone was full of hard-nosed cons who were ready, willing and able to take advantage of a young greenhorn. But not this one. Being bullied and hassled was a thing of the past for me. When you first enter a prison, you soon become aware that jail is run according to a pecking order. There are the scum-bags, the outcasts, who are the child molesters and rapists who no one wants to be associated with. Next up the ladder are the mediocre prisoners, the petty thieves and the two-bob merchants. They're not scum-bags, they're not tough guys, they're not anybody; in fact, they are totally insignificant. Then there is the hierachy: the guv'nors, the tough guys who run the prison. They are the murderers, the bank robbers and gangsters. I was certainly not a scum-bag, and there's no way I was insignificant, so somehow I fitted in with the big boys and they took to me, I felt they accepted me. I wasn't frightened of anyone, and they recognised this in me. I was one of their own – one of the chaps.

I settled down to prison routine. I wouldn't take any shit from anyone, I accepted my lot and, before I knew it, a year had gone by in the blink of an eye. And things were ticking along just fine and dandy until Christmas 1957, just two days before the prison pantomime *Ali Baba and the Forty Thieves*!

It was just another boring day on C Wing. The main event of the day – eating our dinner – was over, and there was nothing to do until lock-up at 8.00pm. Everyone was standing about on the landing, having a fag and chatting, with nothing much out of the ordinary happening.

Then, Joe Mayber, a long-term prisoner and kitchen worker, staggered on to the landing singing at the top of his voice, 'Show me the way to go home ...'

Everyone clocked him and started laughing. One of the

screws began to usher him into his cell, while Joe put his arm round the screw's shoulder and sang in his ear, 'All I want for Christmas is me two front teeth ...' A chorus of prisoners joined in and echoed, 'Me two front teeth ... Me two front teeth ...'

Joe Mayber had clearly helped himself to the methylated spirits from the kitchen. Joe was so obviously pissed, he stunk of meths, and if anyone had thrown a cigarette butt in his direction he would have exploded.

It was just before lock-up, and the prison officer managed to get Joe back to his cell just before he passed out. Later that night, the prison doctor had to be called because Joe was screaming in agony. The doctor couldn't understand why Joe was writhing around in so much pain. At first he thought it was Joe's appendix, then maybe an ulcer. His limbs were shaking uncontrollably, and he was vomiting. The doctor shook his head and diagnosed alcoholic poisoning, and Joe was rushed to the nearby hospital for emergency treatment.

The following morning, there was hell to pay. The Governor wanted answers and someone's head was going to roll; the screws were running around like headless chickens. The Governor was angry, fearing the story would be leaked to the press. Questions needed to be answered. How did Joe Mayber get drunk? Where did he get the alcohol? And, more importantly, was there a breach of security? The prison went on shut-down and we were on lock-up for the next 48 hours.

On the day of the pantomime, preparations were in full swing. Everyone was involved. Ali Baba had his basket and the forty thieves were ready. I and a couple of mates were given the job of working backstage moving the scenery. A red band prisoner who worked in the Roman Catholic chapel managed to smuggle out two bottles of red wine from the Holy Communion cupboard. We sat down amongst the cardboard camels and drank that wine so fast it didn't touch the sides. By that time we had a taste for more and convinced the kid to get us another couple of bottles. Well, if he was going to be caught for two bottles of wine then he might as well be nicked for another couple.

It was now late afternoon and everyone assembled in the hall as the pantomime started – all the cons, the screws, the Governor and local dignitaries were in the audience. No one took much notice of us, they were too busy with the preparations and first night nerves. We, on the other hand, were still messing around in the wings and were so drunk we could barely stand.

The curtain went up. Billy Manning, a robber serving seven years, and I tried to keep quiet, but when an Arthur Mullard lookalike who was playing Ali Baba, pulled out his jewelled dagger and, in a cockney accent, growled, 'Open, says-me,' instead of 'Open, Sesame,' it was just too much for me to take – I howled with laughter.

We continued drinking and by 8.00pm I was as drunk as ten men. I walked back to my cell trying to act normal, not realising that I was wobbling about all over the place. One of the screws noticed my odd behaviour and thought I had been on the methylated spirits just like Joe, and not wanting to lose his job or be held responsible if I was taken ill in the night, he raised the alarm.

At 10.00pm my cell door was flung open, and in walked two screws and a doctor. I was lying face down on my bunk, still fully dressed. I opened one eye and slurred, 'What the fuck do you lot want? If you're after a Christmas drink then you're too late. I've drunk it all.'

I thought my remark was funny; they didn't.

'Stand up, Shaw,' one of them ordered.

I was laughing and staggered to my feet. The doctor ordered me to stick my tongue out, and I told him to fuck off. One of the screws punched me in the guts and winded me. I stopped laughing, it wasn't funny any more. I was no longer in the festive mood. I felt an adrenalin rush shoot through my body, and leaping to my feet I whispered, 'You shouldn't have done that. Now, I'm gonna rip your fucking face off.' I grabbed the officer by the collar and nutted him, making him fall backwards on to the doctor and out of the cell.

As the door slammed in my face, I felt a rage burning inside. How dare he fucking hit me? Who the fuck does he think he is? What the fuck did I do? Did he think by locking me in the cell I couldn't get at him? Did he think he was safe?

I screamed, 'When I get out of here you are going to be sorry, because I'm coming after you and hell is coming with me.'

I kicked the cell door.

'Open the fucking door, you slags.'

Nobody took any notice, I kept kicking the door and shouting. They blanked me. They fucking blanked me, but if they thought I was going to give in they were wrong. I started smashing up the furniture in my cell. In those days, in addition to a bed you had a big heavy chair in the cell. I flung the chair against the wall, smashing it to pieces. I grabbed the seat of the chair and bashed the spy hole in the door.

'Open the fucking door, you slags. When I get out, I'll fucking kill the lot of you.'

Alcohol fuelled my rage and I continued smashing and smashing at the door. I was like a madman, the adrenalin rush made me so strong, I felt I could knock down the walls of a city. I had to get out, it was like a burning obsession. I had to get out of that cell, I was so angry I felt I could kill. I hit the door with one almighty crash, catching the spy hole with the corner of the chair; it broke the glass. I hit the door again and again, and this time the cast-iron support caved in. I clobbered the door so hard that the metal started to split, and soon there was a gaping hole just big enough for me to climb through.

I ran along the deserted landing. The other cons were locked in their cells, screaming and hollering with delight that I'd got one over on the system. The screws were nowhere to be seen. I ran downstairs to a pal of mine called Freddie Samson, who was in an observation cell. He told me to get back into my cell or else I would get into trouble. I laughed, 'Get into trouble? I've just ripped the fucking door off my cell.' Freddie's cell overlooked the main gate, and he could see the screws preparing to storm the wing. He saw the riot shields, the truncheons and the dogs as they prepared to take me on. He pleaded with me to give myself up, but I was pumping; nothing was going to stop me now. I went to the top of the landing where the fire buckets of sand and water were held. I positioned them round the top of the stairs ready to pour the contents over the screws.

The riot squad came on to the wing mob-handed, unaware of the situation they were walking into. I peered over the top of the steel girders and waited until they were in position, then I emptied the sand and water over the top of the landing and, just for good measure, I threw the buckets at them, too. There was sand and water everywhere; it looked like Brighton beach. The riot squad were slipping and sliding and falling over each other. A few managed to scramble up the stairs, and began to chase me. Without thinking, I ran one way and they followed. I was still clutching a chair leg in my hand, it was my only weapon. The screws cornered me. I stopped, turned, raised the chair leg in my hand and gave out a cry of defiance and ran towards them. Instinctively, they turned on their heels and ran back the other way. Then they stopped, turned and chased me. To an onlooker it must have looked like a scene from The Keystone Cops.

Prisoners were banging on their cell doors shouting, 'LEAVE HIM ALONE.' It was complete mayhem. Then the Governor was called, which was unheard of at 10.30 at night. He stood on the landing and witnessed the bedlam that was unfolding around him. At the top of his voice he shouted, 'SHAW, STOP THIS NONSENSE NOW.'

An unnerving silence fell across the landing, and for a second or two everybody stopped what they were doing. He continued. 'IF YOU COME DOWN NOW, I WILL DEAL WITH YOU PERSONALLY IN THE MORNING.'

I knew this meant I would only get 14 days extra on my sentence, it was as much as a Governor's powers could permit, but if it went the full distance I knew I would get an extra six months. I shouted out to the other prisoners,

'DID YOU HEAR THAT EVERYBODY?'

'YEAH,' they answered. 'WE HEARD THAT, ROY.'

The Governor was true to his word. I did 14 days in the punishment block then I was shipped off to Canterbury Prison. They couldn't handle me there, and moved me almost immediately to Pentonville in London.

Whilst at Pentonville I met three of the most feared men in the prison system: Mad Frankie Fraser, Jimmy Andrews and Jimmy Essex. None of the three were big muscle men but they were feared, because if you were foolish enough to fuck with them it would only be a matter of time before they would be back to cut your throat. Make no mistake, they were ruthless, vicious men.

Dinner time at Pentonville was the highlight of the day. On one occasion, I was queuing in the dinner line with Jimmy Essex, as we collected our tin trays and, as usual, moaned about what was for dinner. Another con elbowed his way in front of Jimmy as if we were invisible. Jimmy got the needle. He tapped the geezer on the shoulder and motioned with his thumb to get back. The bloke turned and looked. Jimmy didn't seem to pose a threat to anyone; he didn't look as if he could even have a row, as he was a small, middle-aged man with a bald head and glasses. The con looked Jimmy up and down and said, 'Go away, you old plonker.'

I looked at Jimmy, who glared at the geezer and smiled. 'An old plonker, am I?'

He put his dinner tray down, and went back to his cell. When he returned to the queue, he winked at me, tapped the geezer on the shoulder again and said, 'An old plonker, am I?' He hit the man so hard in the face with a salt pot in a sock that it knocked him sparko. Later, I heard that Jimmy Essex was found guilty of murder while he was still in prison, and it didn't surprise me because Jimmy was a man whose dignity far outweighed his principles.

The same could be said for Fraser and Andrews. Jimmy Andrews was a proud man, a man of honour, but unfortunately was shot dead soon after his release from prison. All three were wicked men, but men who demanded respect. My and Mad Frankie Fraser's paths crossed a few times while we were in prison. We got into so much trouble that at one time the Home Office had stamped on our records: SHAW AND FRASER MUST NEVER BE IN THE SAME PRISON EVER AGAIN.

*   *   *

The time I spent in Pentonville with Fraser, Essex and Andrews was a wild, crazy time. I got into all sorts of trouble, I was running wild. I was full of rage at everything and everyone, furious with society so I lashed out in rage – I attacked screws, grasses, nonces, you name it, I did them all. I took great delight in hurting the child molesters. The authorities knew it was me but had no evidence. All they could see was this violent young man, and all they could do was send me to a psychiatric wing. It was so obvious there was something wrong, I was sent to the psychiatric wing in Wormwood Scrubs to finish off my sentence.

It was April 1959 when I said my goodbyes to the other prisoners on the landing and stepped through the main gates of the prison out into the big wide world. My mate, Albert Rainbird, was waiting, sitting in a big red American car. The hood was down and he was leaning back nonchalantly in a plush white leather seat. He honked the horn as if I hadn't noticed him. As I got in, I joked, 'Nice motor. What is it, the getaway car?'

We laughed and shook hands. I felt excited about being out.

'Where are we going, Albert?'

Albert took me to a nice little Maltese restaurant he knew in Aldgate. It was good to be free once again. We sat in the restaurant enjoying a drink, and I was feeling pretty good; the only thing missing was a woman. I'd been locked up for three years without female company, so when the waitress leaned over my shoulder to put my drink down on the table, I noticed she smelt sweet. I took a deep breath and held it. She smelt of violets.

Albert looked at me with a knowing look that only another man would recognise. I couldn't take my eyes off the young waitress. I looked at her beautiful olive skin and jet-black hair. As she laid the table her hand brushed against mine and sent shivers down my spine. I asked her name but she shied away; she was probably no older than 17. She disappeared into the kitchen so I asked another waiter her name. 'Carolina Debono,' he answered. I melted. My stomach flipped over, I felt like I had been hit by lightning. Bang. I was in love for the first time.

Every day for the next week I went back to the restaurant just to see Carolina. She was the only thing on my mind day and night. I went to bed thinking about her and woke up thinking about her. I kept asking her if I could take her out. She was so innocent, so naïve, at first she said no, but the more she resisted, the more I wanted her. Slowly I won her trust, we became friends, and I started courting her in the old-fashioned way. We got on so well, she was everything I needed at that time, so innocent, so pure, so childlike. I wanted to give her everything, I wanted to spoil her, but it's all very well being in love and wanting to pay for everything – it takes money. I had to work and I don't mean a job that paid a pittance as I had no intention of putting a pound a week away in the Post Office. The only alternative was villainy; a bit of skulduggery, the only thing I knew how to do. So I got in with a little firm doing some nice little blags.

We were an eight-handed firm, all playing our part in making it a success. It started by standing outside a bank to keep watch on the comings and goings of the local firms and factories who collected money for the wages. It was soon established that Wednesday was the day they usually collected the money to get the pay packets ready for Friday. Regular as clockwork each week, the same faces arrived, same time, same place. We watched them put the bags of money in the boots of their cars, then drive off back to their factories. It was then we'd hit them, it was so easy; it was the *Dixon of Dock Green* days.

Our firm was good. Everyone had their own speciality, something they were good at, we were a team and everyone's job was as important as the next. There were the look-outs who made sure the Old Bill weren't sniffing about; the anchor man, he was the one who stayed behind to make sure everyone got away; the men in the ramming car, whose job was to stop the target car at whatever cost. Then there was Albie Yellop, his job was to open the boot of a car and grab the money bags, he was the best at his job and could have a boot open in seconds. My job was to stop the car and dish out any violence if necessary. I used to stand on a corner wearing a rolled-up balaclava holding a house brick wrapped in newspaper under my arm and with an Indian club hidden up my sleeve. I looked like an ordinary working man standing on the corner waiting to be picked up until, that is, the car containing the money left the bank.

As soon as the car was in view, I rolled down my balaclava, ran into the middle of the road and threw the housebrick through the windscreen of the oncoming car. From a side-road the ramming car would smash into the side of the vehicle, stopping it dead in its tracks. I would run up to the car, swing my Indian club into my hand and threaten the passengers, telling them not to move and they wouldn't get hurt. By the time I'd said that, Albie Yellop would have the boot open, and the money in his sticky paws. The poor, unsuspecting workers wouldn't know what had hit them.

We were good at the blags. We travelled all over the country and were riding high. I had a nice car, a nice few quid in my pocket and a beautiful girl I adored. Life couldn't have been better until a Sunday night out that turned into a nightmare.

Carolina and I had met up with Albert Rainbird and Lenny Ketley for a farewell drink because we'd planned a trip to Malta to see Carolina's family. We'd enjoyed a lovely evening, and on the way home through the East End, Lenny suggested stopping off at Bernstein's Bakery in Christian Street, Stepney, for a beigel, a bread roll, which was a Jewish speciality.

It was a Sunday night, we were laughing and joking, we had drank too much, making us a bit worse for wear, but we weren't looking for trouble. I politely asked the lady behind the counter if I could have some extra butter, but I was refused. I asked again, and still she refused. I got annoyed, leapt over the counter and helped myself. She screamed blue murder. Anyone would have thought I was trying to rob the place. The baker heard the commotion and appeared holding a knife, telling us to clear off. I didn't like his attitude and I didn't like him brandishing a knife in front of Carolina. In my world, if you have a knife, you have to be prepared to use it, and in front of my girl isn't a good place to start.

I didn't think about it. I whacked the baker, who fell down and I grabbed the knife. Two other staff members appeared and I ordered them to line up against the wall. I decided there and then I would rob the bakery – after all, I was the one with the knife now. I picked the baker up off the floor and ordered him to line up with the others. Lenny and Albert joined in and emptied the money from the cash tills into their pockets. At that moment, six cab drivers came into the bakery, so I ordered them to line up against the wall as well. It was almost like the 'good old days' of train robbers. We never intended it to be a serious robbery, we were still half-pissed. I waved the knife around in the air. 'This is a stick-up,' I laughed.

I held open a brown paper bag, one used for the beigels, and walked along the line demanding their money and watches. I took a wallet, a watch and a ring from one driver, but I didn't believe it was all he had, and told him, 'If I find anything else in your pockets, I'll chop your fucking head off.'

I put my hand in his jacket pocket expecting to find his night's takings but the driver retaliated by picking up a chair that was close by and bashed me over the head with it. I turned on him, threw him to the floor and started beating him. It was all getting out of hand; Carolina was screaming, and I knew it was time to go. I threw the knife on the counter and we all went to leave, but as we ran out one of the taxi drivers picked up the knife and threw it. It hit Lenny Ketley on the head splitting it wide open, knocking him senseless. We picked him up and helped him into the car, with blood everywhere.

We drove off at high speed. It wasn't meant to be like this, a celebration drink that had gone wrong. We were professional robbers doing professional jobs for Christ's sake, now we were being hunted down for a poxy bit of butter – how did it ever get this crazy?

Unbeknown to us, our registration number had been reported to the police and it wasn't long before they picked us up. I was arrested and charged with ten counts of robbery, and was taken to Brixton Prison to await trial. Prison was the last thing I wanted. I'd promised Carolina I would take her to Malta, she was the most important person in my life and I thought if I went away for a long time, I might lose her. I had just served three years and knew I didn't have a chance in hell of avoiding a custodial sentence. I thought if I did my nut and smashed the cell, then I would have a medical report to say I wasn't responsible for my actions and perhaps receive a lesser sentence – well, anything was worth a try. I remembered back to Maidstone when I smashed my way out of my cell. I decided to try my luck again.

I started smashing up the cell. I bashed the spy hole with a broken chair, and when that didn't work, I used the bed frame to break it, as I knew it would eventually, making a hole big enough to get my head through. I poked my head out on to the landing to see who was about. This time the screws were waiting with their truncheons drawn. They bashed the fuck out of my head. When I pulled my head back into the cell it was streaming with blood. The cell door opened, the screws rushed in, and started to beat me, hitting me with their batons on the arms, shoulders and body.

My skin was splitting and blood poured from the wounds, although I didn't feel a thing because I was so angry that my adrenalin was pumping. I fought hammer and tongs, as though I was fighting for my life. I was in a corner, with my head down and my arms up, swinging punches and kicking, the officers' truncheons were raining down on me, but still I wouldn't give in. Out of the blue, one of the officers yanked my pants and trousers down. I was exposed. I was vulnerable. By pulling down my trousers it took away my shield, it left me defenceless. I felt such a berk standing there with my trousers around my ankles, for a moment I stopped fighting. Then the screws took the opportunity to overpower me. I was dragged down to the strong box, and once inside the screws set about me, only this time I suffered horrific injuries sufficient enough for the prison doctor to be called. My injuries were bad and although the doctor tried his best to stitch up my wounds, I should have been admitted to hospital. It looked like I'd been run over by a truck.

The next morning, the Governor came to see me. He was shocked by the state of me, but told me to let sleeping dogs lie. I could have my medical report and stay in the hospital wing until my trial. At the end of the day I got what I wanted and who was going to believe me anyway? The screws could have said anything, so I agreed and said nothing.

I appeared at the Old Bailey in December 1959 and pleaded guilty to the charges. I only received 21 months' imprisonment because of my hard-earned medical report. Albert Rainbird got 14 months and Lennie Ketley got probation.

I was sent to Wandsworth Prison in London and was allocated a job in the mailbag shop. In those days, you were not allowed to talk, so you learnt to speak out of the corner of your mouth, which is probably why so many gangsters talk that way. In the mailbag shop I sat next to Jack 'The Hat' McVitie, notorious as a fearless brawler who, in the summer of 1967, was offered a spell of employment by the Kray twins. For reasons only known to himself, he cheated the Krays out of some money. To prove his loyalty to Reg and Ron, he was told to shoot Leslie Payne, a former business associate of the Krays. He was given a gun and an advance of £100, with another £400 to follow on completion of the job. Jack never did kill Leslie Payne but, again, he kept the Kray's money. Matters grew worse when Jack got drunk and, armed with a sawn-off shotgun, went to the Regency club in Hackney claiming he was going to shoot Reg and Ron.

On Saturday, 28 October 1967, Jack 'The Hat' was lured to a flat where Reg Kray was waiting. Reggie put his gun against Jack's head and pulled the trigger, but the gun failed to fire. Reg then grabbed Jack, but he managed to struggle his way free and tried to throw himself through a window. He was hauled back by his legs. Reggie took a carving knife and stabbed Jack until he was dead. The rest is history.

Jack 'The Hat' and I became friends as I did my time with him in Wandsworth. He was good company, I got to know him well and I don't think he deserved to die like a dog.

You could always rely on Jack in a fight, like the time in Wandsworth when I planned to hurt a grass. The bastard had turned Queen's evidence, and now because of him, an old mate of mine was doing a ten-stretch. I decided that for the grass, it was pay-back time.

We were watching *Brief Encounter* starring Trevor Howard and Celia Johnson in the prison church. I remember the film so well. It had been shown so often, all the cons knew it word for word. It got to the part where Trevor Howard knew their affair was over and with typical British reserve whispered to Celia Johnson, 'I love you.'

The room echoed with Trevor's words from the motley bunch of cons. They chorused, 'I love you.'

Celia's chin quivered as she replied, 'I know.'

The chorus echoed, 'I know.'

With that I decided it was now or never if I was going to hurt the grass, so I grabbed my chance. I slipped a knife down my sleeve, the blade glinting in the light from the film projector. I put my arm around the grass's neck and pulled him towards me. I could smell tobacco on his breath and saw the fear in his eyes as I plunged the knife deep into his back. He gave out a piercing scream. The lights came on, the screws ran in, and McVitie head-butted the projectionist to take the onus off me. Other prisoners joined in the fight and distracted the screws by overturning the church benches, and all hell broke loose. The grass was lying face down on the floor with the knife still in his back. I walked away nonchalantly. He was a no-good grass and deserved everything he got, so no one should shed any tears for him.

It was common knowledge I'd stabbed the grass but nobody would testify against me. The authorities couldn't prove anything, try as they might. I did a bit of chokey but it was worth it, the grass was in a bad way, and was on the danger list for a while, but he didn't die – unfortunately.

I was moved to 'H' Wing and it was there that I met Frank 'Mad Axeman' Mitchell, another future victim of Reg and Ron's. Frank approached me on 'H' Wing; he was a huge, powerful, good-looking young man, built like an ox, and from the moment I met him we became friends. He had a walk and a talk about him, always eager to please and a lovely guy. When we met he was serving three years for assault. Frank was a right handful, none of the screws could handle him, he would rip their heads off sooner than look at them, so eventually he was nutted off to Broadmoor. Whilst there he escaped with an axe and broke into a house to steal clean clothes. That's how he got his nickname the 'Mad Axeman'. Once he was captured, because he wasn't insane, Broadmoor refused to take him back. He was too dangerous to be released back into society so he was given a life sentence and sent to Dartmoor Prison indefinitely, until, that is, 12 December 1966, when the Kray twins sprung Frank Mitchell from Dartmoor Prison. Mitchell was needed by the twins for a job they had planned. The idea of springing Mitchell from a secure prison was much simpler than it sounded because Mitchell became a trusted prisoner outside on the moors. Before the prison authorities realised Mitchell was missing, he'd been driven to a safe flat in Barking, East London. There he stayed for the next 12 days.

However, Frank became more frustrated at finding himself cooped up with even less freedom than he had when he was in Dartmoor. As Christmas approached, Frank was becoming a nuisance, his demands far outweighing his usefulness and he was becoming a thorn in the twins' sides. They had two choices: give in to his outrageous demands or kill him.

On Christmas Eve 1966, a thin, chilling rain fell as a blue Comer van pulled up outside the flat. An unsuspecting Mitchell got in the van, and he was never seen again. I know for a fact he was shot dead, and I also know who by. But I'm not going to say who did it.

I was in the next cell to Frank Mitchell, and on the same landing as us was a grass, a dirty, stinking grass who'd given information to the authorities about a friend of mine. Whenever I came face to face with the dirty mongrel on the landing, he looked me in the eye. I told Frank I was going to take care of him and today was the day. I collected a broom from the store cupboard and hammered a six-inch nail through it. We waited until everyone was in the exercise yard. Frank and I positioned ourselves behind the grass, and he was completely unaware of what was about to happen as he talked to his friend. The only thing on my mind was to hurt him, and hurt him bad. I felt my hand tighten around the broom handle. As I got close to him, my pace quickened. I swung the broom handle in the air and brought it down with enormous force, plunging my makeshift knife deep into his back. He lunged forward and let out a gasp, unaware he'd been stabbed.

He turned to look at me, with a questioning expression on his face.

'Sorry, mate,' I said casually, and continued to walk around the exercise yard with Frank. The grass was walking in front of us with the broom handle sticking out of his back, and blood began seeping through his blue-striped prison shirt. I smiled at Frank, and walked away confident in the knowledge I had hurt him. Another prisoner tapped the grass on the shoulder and pointed to the broom handle that was sticking out of his back.

As soon as he saw it, he went into shock and fainted. Shortly after that, Frank Mitchell was moved out of Wandsworth into another prison and I never saw him again.

By a strange twist of fate, the next prisoner I met on the landing at Wandsworth Prison was George Cornell. George was a small, vicious little man whom I helped out when three geezers set about him in his cell while he was serving three years for assault. We got our revenge but George wasn't satisfied with that. After the fight, he wanted to settle the score himself. He wanted to torture them for taking a liberty with him. Ironically, George became one of the chief torturers for the Richardson brothers, who were the greatest rivals of Reggie and Ronnie Kray. On 9 March 1966, Ronnie Kray murdered George Cornell in the Blind Beggar pub after a gangland feud.

It wasn't until writing this book some 30 years later that I became aware of the most bizarre set of circumstances involving three men all with the same destiny.

It was while I was in Wandsworth serving 21 months that I met the three ill-fated men: Jack 'The Hat' McVitie, Frank 'The Mad Axeman' Mitchell, and George Cornell – and the one thing they had in common? All three were to die at the hands of the Kray twins.

CHAPTER 5

NICK-KNACK-
PADDY-WHACK

'I tried to keep on the straight and narrow but, once again, the powers that be, the faceless men in the establishment, had decided my destiny for me. I had no alternative but to take the only other path open to me – villainy ...'

I'D SERVED MY 21 MONTHS FOR ROBBING A BAKERY, of all things, and on my release from Wandsworth, I was determined never to be arrested for such a ridiculous offence again.

I'd watched Carolina weep at the Old Bailey when I was sentenced, and it broke my heart to see her cry. Before the robbery, I had promised to take her to Valletta in Malta to see her family. She'd been looking forward to it so much and I had ruined it through my temper. But a promise was a promise – and I intended to fulfil it. In any case, I needed a break myself; violence had become a way of life to me, I'd been in a male-dominated environment and I needed some sun on my back and fresh air in my lungs. I'd been locked up breathing in the stale air of confinement for too long.

I booked two open tickets to Malta. In 1961 they cost me 13 guineas, which to the working man was a lot of money, perhaps a week's wages. To me, it was loose change. I'd stashed away enough dough from the robberies to last for months, I had no need to work, and no need to return home in the immediate future.

We flew from Heathrow to Malta in a small plane. It was the first time I'd travelled by air, and I have to admit to feeling nervous. I sat in a cramped seat, in front of which was a heavy-duty curtain on brass rings. The air hostess walked through the curtain and, to my surprise, I saw the pilot who looked just like Biggles; all he was missing was the white silk scarf. It just added to my anxiety.

I ordered a double vodka to calm my nerves and settled back with Carolina next to me. She was excited about seeing her family and chatted for the whole journey, and it made me so glad to see her happy. Me? I drank my way to Malta!

We stayed in a small village called Qormi just outside Valletta with Carolina's family. The whole country was steeped in religion; statues of the Virgin Mary dominated every house and every bar – in fact, they were absolutely everywhere.

I found the Roman Catholic religion to be very strict; there are rules for just about everything, from the use of contraceptives to abortion, and unmarried couples are certainly not allowed to sleep together. I'd been in prison for nearly two years, unable even to touch a woman, and now I was free and in a beautiful country, enjoying the company of the woman I loved, but still unable to sleep with her unless we were married. I was caught between the devil and the deep blue sea. I'm not sure if it was the hot sun that affected my brain or if I'd been carried away by the romance of it all, or maybe I just wanted my wicked way, but I did the gentlemanly thing – I proposed to Carolina.

On 21 August 1961, we married in a small Roman Catholic church in Malta. The memory of Carolina floating down the aisle whilst 'Ave Maria' echoed around the church still remains with me today. Carolina was a vision of loveliness; she was so pure, so precious. I desired her so much. Three months earlier I'd been locked in a stinking prison cell, and now I was just about to marry the woman of my dreams – my Carolina. I wanted to savour every moment. I looked around at the shimmering stained-glass windows, and at the priest rhythmically swinging his censer to and fro. I smiled. I watched the Mediterranean widows dressed in black, kneeling in front of the altar clutching their rosary beads. I swallowed hard and realised I was the luckiest man alive.

After the ceremony, we walked hand in hand through the narrow cobbled streets with the whole congregation following. We went to a local bar for a celebratory drink, our spirits high; we were madly in love. I made sure everyone had a drink in their hand for the toast, and then I raised my glass.

'Has everyone got a drink?' I called.

Attached to the door of the bar was a huge statue of the Virgin Mary. The bar fell silent for the toast. I raised my glass, pointed to the statue, and joked, 'Oh look, she hasn't got a drink.'

On the spur of the moment, for a laugh, I threw my drink in the face of the statue. The ice cubes and vodka splashed against the image of the Virgin Mary. There were gasps from the guests. A hushed silence fell across the bar, and Carolina's jaw dropped open.

As soon as I had done it, I realised I had offended them and had insulted their religion. It wasn't a good start to the marriage, as Carolina burst into tears. I was amazed at her reaction. I wasn't used to pussy-footing around, or dealing with women's feelings. I had no idea what to say or do. Carolina forgave me, but I don't think her family ever did. I didn't really give a fuck what they thought, I had got what I wanted – Carolina.

We were inseparable, going everywhere together. By day, we lay on the sun-drenched beach, soaking up the sun, but as night fell we visited the bars and restaurants around the small fishing villages. There is nothing quite like an evening out on holiday in a hot country. As the sun goes down, after washing, shaving and putting on a crisp white shirt, walking past the street cafés and bars and breathing in the balmy night air, it's a unique feeling, the ultimate feel-good factor.

Carolina pressed my white shirt and laid it out on the bed for me. We'd planned to go out for an evening to Valletta and her sister was coming with us. First, we'd be stopping off at a local bar for an early evening drink, and then going on to a restaurant for dinner. We arrived at the Kestrel Bar, which was packed, and

I told the girls to find an empty table and elbowed my way to the bar. I stood at the counter ordering our drinks with my eye on the girls who had settled at a candle-lit table covered with a red gingham tablecloth. I tried not to take my eyes off them because I felt very protective towards my new bride. In the time it took to order and pay for the drinks, I glanced back to the table and surrounding the girls were three British sailors who were chatting up my wife and her sister.

I left the drinks on the counter and went back to where the girls were sitting, intent on making it clear to the sailors that the girls were with me. I tapped one of them on the shoulder and, without looking round, he said, 'Push off, mate, we were here first.'

Fucking liberty. I grabbed the back of his head and smashed his face down on to the table. He was out cold. Before the other two had a chance to say anything, I whacked the second sailor, who fell backwards taking the red gingham tablecloth with him. I was just about to wallop the third one when the owner of the bar rushed over to try and stop the fight by jumping on my back. He was a landlord well used to running a bar full of sailors, sorting out the scraps that happened nightly. To him, it was just another fight, he wasn't bothered, he was ready and willing to take on Popeye the Sailor Man if necessary.

The landlord was on my back with his arms around my neck in a vice-like grip. I managed to throw him over my shoulder on to the floor, smashing glasses and bottles as he landed. My argument wasn't with him so I leant over to help him to his feet and was rewarded with a fist full in the face. Automatically, I head-butted him, and down he went again, this time completely sparko. In knocking out the owner, I had inadvertently insulted the locals who were drinking in the bar. It ended up in a right old tear-up. I started to knock a few of them out, and as soon as I put one down then another came at me. They were all hooting and hollering and making one hell of a din. Carolina was frightened, and she said they were going to kill me. She screamed at them to leave me alone.

The largest of them puffed his chest out and said, 'Try me for size, you short English bastard.' So I did, and knocked him out. The police arrived and fearing I would be lynched by the angry mob decided to get me out of the bar and into a nearby bus shelter for safety. The crowd wasn't satisfied with that and followed, surrounding the bus shelter and baying for my blood. I was in the middle of two policemen, who thought they had the situation under control until the angry mob started to rock the shelter to and fro. The noise was deafening, and when a brick hurtled through the window just missing one of the officers, they realised they were way out of their depth, and couldn't understand how one man could upset an entire village. The Maltese police were not used to dealing with so much anger and violence on a large scale, and didn't seem to know what to do. I offered to sort it out, but the police just saw me as a trouble-making visitor.

One of the officers braved the crowd. He wasn't bothered about the Maltese locals, he knew he could handle them, all he had to do was wave his stick in the air and shout loudly for them to step back in line.

I was charged and taken to the police station (if you could call it that), which was vastly different to police stations back home. It was just like the jail house in a Western film, a brick-built hut with dirt on the floor and an iron bed in the corner that was alive with bed bugs.

I was taken into a small room to be interviewed, the officers behaved themselves all the time my wife was in the room, but as soon as she left they set about me with their truncheons.

Truncheons back home were wooden and if you got whacked with one of those it split the skin open, unlike the truncheons used by the Maltese which were made out of bamboo. The officers set about me viciously. Their truncheons fucking hurt, and left reddened weals all over my head, back and face. I looked like I'd been flogged with a cat-o'-nine-tails.

I was slung back into the cell and laid on the bed, deprived of every creature comfort other than the creatures who shared my bed. Enough was enough. I banged on the cell door until the guard arrived. He leered at me, and through his gold-tooth smile and garlic breath said, 'Bastard, look what you have done to me. You have ripped my shirt.'

'Ripped your shirt? Look what you've done to me,' I answered.

I pointed to my body and the weals that had now developed into bruised purple lines resembling an Ordnance Survey map. He turned away with utter disdain, and walked back to his half-eaten supper.

In the morning, things were different. The attitude of the police towards me had changed overnight. They were no longer hostile, in fact they were falling over themselves to shake my hand and pat my back. It was unnerving, that suddenly everything had changed so dramatically. I was no longer the bad guy; instead, I was a celebrity. The bar owner dropped all the charges, and even my wife's brother came from another village just to shake my hand.

I decided to go back to the Kestrel Bar to find out the reason for the turn-around. Why was everybody being so nice to me? I'd smashed up one of their bars, knocked out a few locals and insulted the police. All of a sudden I'm fucking Superman. It wasn't right.

Call me an old cynic, but I had to get to the bottom of it. I walked into the Kestrel alone. The way I figured it, if anyone had anything to say, there I was, larger than life and on my own. Immediately, I was surrounded by the locals all wanting to shake my hand and buy me a drink. I was paranoid. I thought they were trying to get me drunk and then use the opportunity to hurt me. Even the police who had arrested me the night before came into the bar to shake my hand. I'd become a celebrity – and a paranoid celebrity. I shook their hands and drank their drinks, and all of a sudden I had an army of mates – but I wasn't stupid, I knew their little game. At least I thought I did. So I drank all the drinks bought for me, but unbeknown to them, I then went into the toilet and made myself sick.

I thought I was clever, one step ahead of them, but in reality

Let's go to work! Who's next?

Top left: My beautiful Mum – she gave this photo to my Dad.

Top right: My Dad – I still miss him today.

Bottom: I'm in the front row centre, suited and booted even aged fifteen. We were all on our way to box in the ABA Schools' Championships.

I was married to Carolina in Malta. She looked stunning and it was
a happy day.

RED PAROLE CARDS ARE ISSUED FOR SPECIFIC AREAS SUCH AS CENTRE CORRIDOR AND CENTRE YARD AND ARE FOR WORK PURPOSES ONLY.

PAROLE

Parole patients will be allowed to leave their houses unescorted at certain hours and for the undermentioned purposes. They must report to the nurse in charge of the houses when leaving or returning. They must return for all meals and not later than the times laid down for parole.

1. To attend certain work areas, proceeding direct and reporting their arrival and not delaying en route for any reason. They must not interfere with the other House counts. They are not allowed to leave the work area except with permission of the person in charge.

2. To visit the Canteen, Monday, Tuesday, Thursday and Friday without previous notice at agreed times.

3. To visit friends in other Houses, except Norfolk and Monmouth, at times convenient to the Nurse in charge.

4. To visit friends in the airing courts of Essex and Gloucester houses only, at recognised times.

5. To stroll on the terrace. (The bottom walk only during visiting hours.)

6. To have their visits on the terrace. (Talking or mixing with other patient's visitors is not allowed.)

7. The north side of Kent and Dorset houses is not a parole area, except for going to work in the workshops.

This card is issued 5804

to SHAW. R. H

who has been granted Inside Parole

Patient's Signature R Shaw

Date 24. 6. 1969.

Patrick G McGran

Physician Superintendent

Top left: All dressed up and nowhere to go – another day in Broadmoor.

Top right: The wall that I built – in the grounds at Broadmoor.

Bottom: My Broadmoor parole card – the mug shot says it all.

A thoughtful
moment in
the gym.

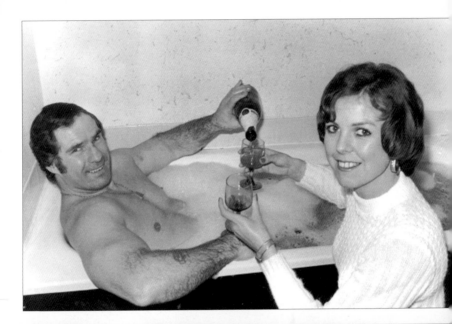

Top: The good life with Dorothy!

Bottom: Another day another win – what a buzz!

osher Powell had just jumped off his chair onto my stomach – all sixteen
tone of him!

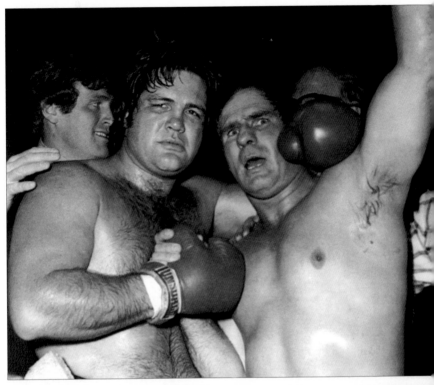

Top: I'd just beaten Ron Stander – the heavy weight World Champion contender and probably my hardest fight.

Bottom: The chaps gathered together for Joe Pyle's son's wedding. From left to right, Tony Lambrianou, me, Joe Pyle, Johnny Hibner, Gerry, Freddie Foreman and Alfie Hutchison.

they weren't trying to get me drunk at all. I was just being suspicious, like the old joke, ''Course I'm not paranoid, but who's that following me?'

From then on, wherever I went, I was shown the utmost respect. Word of my escapade soon spread around the island like wildfire, eventually reaching a club on the other side of the island. Carolina and I had gone on a day trip to St Paul's Bay and were standing in a club enjoying a drink, when a whisper went round that 'Galoore' was coming, the most feared man on the island. Nervous anticipation filled the air, and suddenly the bar emptied. Everybody disappeared. It was like a saloon in a corny Western, when the baddies ride into town. I was a stranger in town; the word 'Galoore' meant nothing to me and I had no intention of moving.

John Wayne could have ridden into town on his trusty steed, with a patch over his eye, holding a gun in each hand, and I still wouldn't have moved.

The saloon door opened, and standing in the doorway with the sun blazing behind him was Galoore, a short, stocky man with no neck and close-cropped hair. For a moment he paused, and scanned the bar. I eye-balled him, he eye-balled me. He moved casually, smiled carefully and spoke slowly, 'You the champion of Malta, me the next best.'

Instantly, I recognised a man of courage. He could have confronted me mob-handed but he didn't, he came alone, and for that reason our respect was mutual and we shook hands. We became friends and he turned out to be the nicest bloke you could ever wish to meet. Galoore had a reputation in Malta. In every bar, every restaurant, Galoore had the best treatment. The best seats. The best food. We were inseparable for the rest of my time in Malta. I witnessed, first hand, the treatment he received. I saw the look in people's eyes wherever he went, and to this day I still don't know if it was a look of respect or fear. There is a difference. If someone likes you out of fear it's a false friendship. If, on the other hand, they like you out of respect, that's different because with respect comes power and I liked it. The lesson I learnt from Galoore was that you earn respect and demand fear.

We stayed in Malta for three glorious months but there is only so much sun, sea and soppy stuff a man can stand, and eventually it was time to go home. Carolina was pregnant and things needed to be sorted.

We returned to England and settled in a small flat in Church Road, Romford, Essex. Carolina was busy preparing for motherhood and I decided to try my hand at boxing again. Boxing was the only thing I ever wanted to do, and if I could get my licence back, I knew I could make an honest career out of it.

I went to see Mickey Duff, who made arrangements for me to go before the British Boxing Board of Control, in an attempt to get my licence back. The Board of Control consisted of QCs, solicitors and top-brass police officers. I stood in front of them while they fired questions at me. They asked what I had been doing for the past three years, and because I was using the assumed name of Roy West I hoped they didn't discover my true identity and that I'd been in prison for the past three years under my real name of Shaw. If they found out about my prison record I wouldn't have a hope in hell of getting my licence back. So I decided to tell them a few porky pies, saying I had been working all over the country, mainly up north. They listened to my story, made a few notes, ummed and ahhed, shuffled their papers and tutted, but I knew in my heart of hearts I wouldn't get my licence back.

A few days later, a letter arrived and my worst suspicions were confirmed – I had been refused my licence. I felt I had been kicked in the stomach; refusing to give me my licence back hurt more than any punch I had ever received. I felt lost. My life was at a cross-roads, and boxing was my only skill.

I tried to keep on the straight and narrow but, once again, the powers that be, the faceless men in the establishment, had decided my destiny for me. I had no alternative but to take the only other path open to me – villainy. I had nothing to lose and I was going into villainy with a vengeance. Once again, I had been stopped from doing what I wanted to do. I was angry, and when I get angry, I get fucking nasty, and boy did I get nasty one night at the Limbo Club in Wardour Mews all because of a cashmere overcoat.

My overcoat was the bollocks. I felt good as I swaggered into the Limbo Club. I handed my overcoat to the doorman and told him to look after it.

'Leave it to me, Roy, I'll hang it up right by the door so I can keep an eye on it.'

I watched as he hung it on a wooden coat hanger, brushed it down and placed it by the front door of the club so it wouldn't be out of his sight for a moment. I sat at my usual table, ordered some drinks and was enjoying a lovely evening out. In the early Sixties, it was unusual to see black faces in a traditional club, it was just the way it was then, and if there were any non-whites in a club they stuck out like sore thumbs.

This particular night, I happened to notice a couple of black men in the club. They didn't bother me, and if they didn't mess with me then I wouldn't mess with them. We were having a good night, the cabaret was good, the music was loud and the alcohol was plentiful. But I kept noticing one of the black men looking at Carolina. It started to bother me but I didn't want to spoil the evening. He was either incredibly brave or incredibly stupid because he totally ignored me and my warning looks.

He strutted towards us wearing a baggy zoot suit and a pork-pie hat. He was a Harlem cat doing the Harlem shuffle. He totally blanked me, never once looking in my direction. Was I invisible? He held his hand out and asked Carolina to dance. I didn't give a fuck what creed or colour he was, no one asked my wife to dance. I grabbed his kipper tie and pulled him towards me and told him to fuck off. A girl standing close by instantly got the hump and piped up, 'Why are you having a go at him? Is it because he's black?'

I told her I didn't give a fuck if he was black, white or purple with yellow spots, he wasn't dancing with my wife. The Harlem cat picked up a bottle from the table and smashed it. Now any fool can pick up a bottle, but if you break a bottle in front of me you've got to be prepared to use it. The doorman clocked what was happening and threw me a cosh, and while the geezer was still thinking about it, I smashed the bottle out of his hand and whacked him across the nut with the cosh. As I hit him, I felt someone jump on my back, and I immediately thought it was one of his mates. I threw him off and realised it wasn't at all; it was a big Irishman telling me, 'Will ya leave the black fella alone?'

I couldn't understand why an Irishman would want to stop me bashing this geezer, particularly as he'd taken a liberty. Now my anger was directed at the Irishman. I hit him once, knocking him sideways, and I continued hitting him all the way towards the door of the club. I gave him one almighty crack, but instead of falling through the door he fell against my overcoat.

I watched in horror as he slid down my coat leaving a trail of blood behind him. Of all the places he could have chosen to bleed on, he picked my new coat. Now I was annoyed.

The police arrived, the Irishman was carted off to hospital and I picked up my blood-stained coat. I was really pissed off – the fight had had nothing to do with the paddy, but he'd decided to put his sticky beak in. I wasn't going to let it go – now it was personal.

I called a taxi and went to Charing Cross Hospital. I told Carolina to stay in the car and for the taxi driver to leave the engine running. I tucked the cosh up my sleeve and walked into the hospital. I enquired about any new admittances and was directed to an examination room through the double doors at the end of the corridor. I peered through the window of the door and saw the big Irishman lying on a table surrounded by doctors and nurses. I waited until they'd left the room, then I walked in. The geezer sat up holding a big piece of gauze to the side of his head and whispered, 'If you've come to apologise ...'

I slid the cosh down my sleeve and walked towards him. I hadn't come to apologise. He looked into my face, then at the cosh and cowered down to protect himself, screaming blue murder as I gave him one last crack. On hearing the blood-curdling screams, the doctors rushed in as I walked out of the other door.

I kicked open a double door which led straight into a geriatric ward with rows of beds on either side. The lights were dim, a solitary nurse sat reading a book at the end of the ward with a night light. A doctor shouted, 'Stop that man.'

An orderly made a grab for me. Bang, I hit him and he went down. On hearing the commotion, the patients started to wake up and call for the nurse. Another man approached me – there always has to be a hero, and this time it was a porter. I swatted him like a gnat and strode down the ward towards the exit, satisfied. Revenge was sweet.

*   *   *

In the early hours of 17 July 1962, Carolina went into labour. I took her to the local hospital and was shown into a side room to wait with the other expectant fathers. The doctor told me it would be hours before the baby arrived, and to come back later in the day. I didn't want to leave her but I had a bit of business to attend to and knew she was in safe hands. I stepped out of the hospital into beautiful hot sunshine, glad to be a man. By late afternoon I returned to the hospital just as the baby was being born. I was taken into the delivery suite, where Carolina was sitting up in bed, looking exhausted. A matron held out a small bundle saying, 'You've got a daughter, Mr Shaw.'

I looked at the baby; she was a tiny little thing with dark skin and a mop of black hair. 'That's not my baby, she's black,' I shouted.

The surly matron snatched the sunglasses from my face. I looked at my baby again, and she no longer looked black. I laughed. The matron didn't. I held my beautiful baby daughter for the first time. We named her Chatina Shaw. I was now a father with responsibilities and Carolina hoped that now I was a father it would calm me down. She was wrong.

Carolina was happy and content playing mother, she had everything she wanted, with nothing to worry about, and so long as I had the money to pay the bills and buy everything for the baby, she asked no questions, so I told her no lies.

I settled back into the world of villainy. The daytime I spent with Carolina and the baby, and by 7.00pm every night I was washed, changed and out with the boys. The pubs and the clubs were my offices. That's where we plotted and planned, where other villains would come in with information on this blag or that blag.

In those days, there was a code of honour amongst villains, we trusted each other and it was a different ball game then. Today, everything revolves around drugs – villainy is motivated by drugs. Addicts will do anything for their next fix. Drugs have changed the face of villainy beyond belief. People lack morals and standards nowadays, drugs have been the downfall of society, where nothing is sacred if people will sell their own grandmother for the price of a fix.

Saturday night is ladies' night in the underworld when gangsters take their wives out. Mum would happily babysit for us as any grandmother would. I took Carolina to the West End and met up with Albert Rainbird and Lenny Ketley and hit the town. By 4.30am we were still buzzing; we'd been to Churchill's, the Astor Club and had gone to Soho looking for another club that was open.

By chance, we came across a seedy little joint in a basement. We decided to try our luck and get in. Lenny and Albert went down first, and I held Carolina's hand as she tried to climb down the stairs in her stiletto heels. I banged on the door. A doorman opened a big shutter and growled, 'Members only.'

I told him not to be a ponce and to let us in. He shrugged his shoulders and opened the door. We walked into the darkness of the club. The air was thick with smoke and the rhythm of the rumba was contagious. I peered through the gloom.

You could cut the atmosphere with a knife. The bad vibes permeated the club like a bad smell – it was instant trouble.

Albert warned me not to start anything or we would all be dead. A girl who was drunk approached us and hissed, 'You flash bastards,' then spat in my face.

A minder came over and told us to leave. I didn't argue with him, I just gave him a slap on the way out. I slammed the door shut behind us and pulled the shutters up. I wasn't silly enough to start any trouble in the club but I wasn't prepared to leave it at that. The others knew I wouldn't. I told Albert to get me the gallon canister of petrol from the boot of the car. Fearing what I might do, he started to protest, 'But, Roy ...'

I was having none of it. 'Just fucking get it ...'

I poured the petrol down the wooden stairs and around the entrance, banged on the door and shouted for the bastards to come out. I ran back up the stairs, and as the shutters opened I threw a match – the club and all its 'members' exploded into a ball of fire.

*   *   *

In the spring of 1963, Carolina became pregnant again. I was still up to no good as far as the blags were concerned, but I had also branched out into the protection racket. I looked after the odd club or two. When I say 'looked after', I mean protected. Every month I would collect a pension from the owner. That way, as long as the pension was paid, there would be no trouble in his club. If I put my name to a place and there was any trouble, it was down to me to sort it. Word soon got round that I wasn't a man to mess with, but there is always someone who wants to take a liberty.

I started looking after a late-night drinking den called The Limbo Club in Wardour Mews in the West End. The Maltese owner of the club phoned me to let me know an Irishman had tried to get a pension from him. He tried to step on my toes, knowing I had the door at the Limbo Club, and he still tried to get a pension from it. I found out that the Irishman was Paddy Mullins, six foot, deep-set – and he'd taken a fucking liberty! It was down to me to sort it. I heard through the grapevine that Paddy was known to carry a knife and wasn't shy of using it. I prepared myself by slipping a hunting knife down the front of my trousers before I walked into the packed club. Mullins was standing at the bar, I appproached him smiling, and asked him what he was drinking.

'Guinness, Paddy?'

He finished the remainder of his pint and nodded. I handed him his drink and continued, 'I think you and me ought to have a little talk.'

It must have been the way I said it because he copped the needle and sneered, 'I haven't got to talk to you about fuck-all. Whatever I do is none of your Goddamn business.'

'None of my Goddamn business? I'M MAKING IT MY FUCKING BUSINESS,' I yelled as he hit the ground.

Normally, when I knock someone down, that's good enough for me, I never follow through with a kicking but there's nothing worse than a paddy with attitude. I pulled the knife from my belt, looked at the serrated edge and thought, Fuck it, why not? I jumped on top of Paddy and yelled, 'NONE OF MY GODDAMN BUSINESS, AIN'T IT?' as I plunged the knife deep into his arse and legs, again and again. He screamed like a stuck pig, and bled like one, too. Before I knew it, the police had arrived and I was charged with GBH.

I was not remanded in custody because my wife was pregnant and alone in a strange country. The baby was due at any moment and if she'd gone into labour and I was in prison she would have had no one to help her. At least that was the excuse I used.

The trial started, and for the first three days I was allowed to return home. Halfway through the trial, the prosecution started presenting their evidence. I was remanded in custody and sent to Brixton Prison. The following day I was taken to the court. Paddy Mullins took the witness stand. The prosecution thought it was a clear-cut case until Paddy said, 'If it wasn't for that man, I'd be dead. He saved my life. He's a hero.'

The entire courtroom was shocked at the turnaround. I wasn't.

No words were necessary. Just a look in Paddy's direction was enough. Maybe calling me a hero was a tad over the top, but he hadn't been so thick after all. I was found not guilty and released.

A mate was waiting to drive me home. We were laughing and joking, unaware of the events of the previous night. I wasn't too concerned that Carolina hadn't been in court to hear the verdict, as I'd already reassured her that everything was going to be OK. As I walked into our block of flats, I met a woman coming out who later turned out to be the midwife. I was happy, smiled and wished her a good morning. She scowled at me, and if looks could kill I'd be stone dead. I thought, Miserable old cow, how could anybody not be happy on a bright, sunny September day? I was even happier when I walked into the flat and saw my wife sitting up in bed holding our baby son, Gary. I rushed out of the flat, leaned over the balcony and called out to my mate, 'IT'S A BOY. I'VE GOT A SON. A BEAUTIFUL BABY BOY.'

I was 27 years old and I had everything a man could want – money, respect, a doting wife and two beautiful children. I was on top of the world. Untouchable, or so I thought. Six weeks after the birth of my son, I was in for a fall, the biggest fall of my life.

CHAPTER 6

AS SURE AS SHAW CAN BE

"Royston Henry Shaw, I am arresting you on suspicion of armed robbery on a security van in Longfield, Kent. You are not obliged to say anything but what you do say will be taken down and used in evidence against you."

'GIMME THE MONEY, and no one gets hurt.' I was hyped up, adrenalin pumping through my body.

'Gimme the fucking money,' I ordered.

The bank employees were like frightened rabbits as they crouched on the floor of the security van. I could smell their fear, almost taste it. There was no question, if they'd moved I would have killed them. I wasn't bothered either way, violence was simply an accepted part of my business.

'Don't hurt us. Take the money,' they pleaded.

I grabbed one of the suitcases. Suddenly, a bank employee looked up. His eyes widened in alarm.

'Not those, they're empty, they're the cases you want,' he gasped as he pointed to a stack of brown suitcases. The moment of truth had arrived. It was the completion of the big robbery we had been carefully planning for the past three months. Everything had gone according to plan; I had the money, and like the missing piece of a jigsaw puzzle it had all slotted into place.

Let me take you back to the beginning. Unbeknown to

Carolina while she was pregnant with our son, I'd been involved in masterminding an armed robbery, one to match the Great Train Robbery that took place on 8 August 1963, when 15 hooded men stopped the Glasgow to London overnight mail train, robbing it of £2,631,684. Until then, Britain's most spectacular robberies had yielded only a fraction of that sum. The Great Train Robbery was an inside job, on that scale it had to be. With the information we had, we realised that, hopefully, our armed robbery on a Martin's Security van would be on the same scale.

The swinging Sixties produced a number of villains whose defiance of law and order earned them a recognition that has sometimes bordered on respect and even admiration. It was a time of peace and love. Technology hadn't taken over, thus enabling shady characters to get up to all sorts of skulduggery.

It had all started with the Great Train Robbery when the public was outraged that a Royal Mail train had been robbed and, worse still, the robbers were still at large. Up until then, long prison sentences were unheard of. A ten-year jail sentence was a rarity, and meted out for only very serious crimes. A 12-year jail sentence was a life sentence, and any sentence above that was capital punishment – a life for a life. After the Great Train Robbery, the Goverment decided to take action and clean up the streets of London, making examples of the offenders. Headlines in the newspapers screamed: LONG SENTENCES ARE HERE TO STAY.

It was an uncompromising warning to the criminal world from the highest judge in the land, that the era of crippling jail sentences for bank robberies and the like were official. Long prison sentences or even capital punishment was not a deterrent to anyone. Take it from me as a convicted criminal myself, I can categorically confirm that while committing any crime you're completely and utterly convinced you are not going to get caught. And when caught, we aren't sorry for the crime, only sorry for the situation we find ourselves in, which is usually prison. It was like that for the armed robbery we planned in Kent on the security van; we were as sure as sure could be that we weren't going to get caught.

For three long months, day in, day out, we systematically planned and calculated every move, strategically organising every detail, leaving nothing to chance, until we thought our meticulous plan was fool-proof.

I followed the security van until I knew the timetable, the route and the days when the money was collected, like the back of my hand. We'd practised the run over and over again, until we were able to pinpoint the best possible place to attack.

On 27 September 1963, at 11.40am, the amoured van passed five professional criminals pretending to play football on a small Kent pitch. We had taken the football to look inconspicuous while we waited for the van to return exactly half an hour later. We knew the time the van was due, having been over our plans time and time again, leaving nothing to chance.

At precisely 12.10pm in broad daylight on a typical, blustery September day, the armoured van came into view as we knew it would. Everyone had taken up their positions. The ramming lorry was parked across the road. Charlie sat in the passenger seat, and John was in the driving seat anxiously tapping his fingers on the steering wheel waiting for me to give him the nod. The jeep was parked on the corner of the T-junction, and hanging from the front bumpers were grappling hooks. Colin sat inside with the engine running, ready to attach the hooks to the security van doors. The ramming lorry's job was to force the armoured van off the road, and the grappling hooks on the jeep were to be attached to the back doors. Colin would then reverse the jeep at speed, ripping the doors clean off, and then unload the money and go. Parked 50 yards up the road was the getaway vehicle, a blue Thames van that had been stolen a few days before. Harry sat in the van nervously smoking a fag, waiting for his cue to go. The original idea of 'rob and go' was really simple, but like many well-laid plans they can sometimes go wrong.

I stood on the corner of the T-junction. My eyes scanned the quiet country lane and beyond to see if the coast was clear. The only sound was the rustling of the trees and the pounding of my heart. I experienced a few moments of unease and doubt. What if this happened? What if that happened? But I pushed them to the back of mind.

As soon as the van came into view, I pulled my balaclava over my face. My hand tightened round a house brick and an Indian club swung on my wrist. Lying close by was an axe which I had sharpened myself that morning.

As the van approached I knew that whatever happened next would alter the course of my life; in the next ten seconds my future was about to change for ever.

I nodded to John in the ramming lorry and looked at Colin sitting in the jeep, 'It's coming, Col, get ready.'

Colin's eyes bulged through the slits in his balaclava as if he had taken an ounce of whizz, but we had no need for illegal substances, we were high on adrenalin. I waited until the van came within spitting distance before hurling the house brick. It went straight through the windscreen, hitting the driver on the head. The van careered out of control. In a split second it all went wrong. Instead of the ramming lorry hitting the security van, I watched in horror as it sailed straight past the security van like ships that pass in the night. I couldn't believe it – the ramming lorry had missed, it had fucking missed.

The van came to an abrupt stop 20 yards up the road. I ran towards it. The terrified driver had blood streaming down his face, and was in a state of shock. I was buzzing, high on adrenalin, breathless with excitement. I felt marvellous, indestructable. I wanted that money and nothing was going to stop me from getting it. I pulled at the driver's door. It was locked. I swung my Indian club into my hand and smashed the window, shattering it into a million pieces. I grabbed the driver by the neck, dragged him through the broken window and slung him in a ditch. The van was now out of action. John, Charlie, Harry and I surrounded the van, banging on the side and screaming for them to open the back, but it was sealed as tight as a tin of sardines.

I ran back to the T-junction to get my axe. No matter what it took, I was going to get into that van. I swung my axe at the side window and, to my great surprise, the barred window disappeared inside, leaving a gaping hole where it had once been. I hauled myself through. Five bank officials cowered in the corner as I yelled, 'GIMME THE MONEY AND NO ONE GETS HURT. GIMME THE FUCKING MONEY.'

'Don't hurt us, take the money,' they pleaded.

Stacked on either side of the van were brown suitcases each two foot long. I grabbed one of the cases and shook it. By the weight of it, I knew it was full. Our inside information was correct; the security van had, indeed, picked up the surplus money from the six banks. I handed one of the cases to the eager, outstretched arms of John, who tossed it to Charlie, who in turn tossed it to Harry, just like a conveyor belt on *The Generation Game* TV show, but there were no toasters or cuddly toys, this was lolly, spondulix, dosh. Lovely, lovely money that was never to be seen again!

By the time I had climbed out of the van, we had an audience of sightseers trying to make themselves busy. I ran at the astonished bystanders yelling at them, warning them to get back. Simultaneously, Colin, fuelled by anger and perhaps a tad over-zealous, jumped back into the jeep and drove towards the crowd. They ran in every direction fearing for their lives, as you would if a raving lunatic charged at you with all guns blazing. I ran to the jeep, grabbed Colin's arm and shouted, 'Leave it, let's get the fuck out of here.'

With the money stashed safely in the back of the van, we sped along the quiet country lane like a bat out of hell. Harry the driver noticed a vehicle following us erratically. We tried to lose him but he remained on our tail which confirmed our suspicions – we were, indeed, being followed.

It was the same old story. People just can't keep their fucking noses out of other people's business. There we had it, yet another hero. I didn't see it as a problem, just as an annoyance.

'Stop the van, Harry, I'll take care of him.'

Harry screeched the van to a halt. I leapt out. My pursuer

stopped his van so quickly it left black tyre marks on the road. Having made his first mistake by following us, he then made his second by stopping. I stood in the middle of the road, and the brave fucking soldier didn't know what to do. We were alone in a country lane, and he'd followed us not giving any thought as to what he might do if he caught us.

There we were, just him and me, face to face. It was a stupid situation, like the nonsense rhyme:

> *One sunny day in the middle of the night,*
> *Two dead men got up to fight,*
> *Back to back they faced each other,*
> *Drew their swords and shot each other.*

I looked at him, he looked at me, and in a moment it dawned on our hero – just what was he going to do? It didn't take him long to decide as I charged at him brandishing my axe.

In his panic he crunched his gears into reverse and careered up the grass bank, his wheels spinning out of control, heaving tufts of grass and mud into the air. Black smoke billowed from the engine. As if in slow motion, I watched the van topple on to its roof, slide down the bank, and end up completely blocking the road, stopping the police or anyone else from tracking us. For once, a hero had done us a favour.

I got back in the van. 'That's fucked 'em, boys. No one can follow us now.'

No one doubted I couldn't take care of our hero. One of the boys laughed and said, 'Are you sure he ain't gonna follow us on foot, Roy? You fucking head-case!'

I humoured him and asked: 'What do you mean by that?'

They all looked at each other and burst out laughing.

We continued to speed down the narrow country lane for about another mile until we reached a coal tipper lorry which had been stolen specially for this job. From the outside, the coal lorry looked like any other, but inside it concealed a secret hiding place. Hidden beneath the layer of coal was a carefully constructed platform made from scaffolding tubes. To any passer-by or nosy copper it looked perfectly ordinary, but in reality it was our getaway lorry. We kicked open the van doors and piled out. Frank, the driver of the coal lorry, jumped out of the cab eager for news, 'Did ya get it? Did you get the money?'

We pulled our balaclavas from our faces. We were hot and sweaty and it felt good to get them off. Frank's eyes lit up when he saw the cases. I had no time even to acknowledge him or for idle chit chat. I stooped underneath the lorry and hauled myself up through a hole that had been cut into the floor. I squeezed myself into the void between the coal and the floor of the truck. Quickly, the others passed the suitcases to me and I stashed them among the scaffold tubes. Once all six cases were safely in place, the rest of the gang scrambled through the hole. One by one they eased themselves into the back of the truck and found a space to crouch beneath the rusty scaffold tubes. Once we were all safely inside, Frank climbed back into the cab and tested our communication system. It actually sounds very sophisticated, but in fact it was several hoover pipes stuck together with electrical tape. This enabled Frank to warn us if there were any Old Bill around. When Colin told us his idea to use the hoover pipes after watching a film about submarines, we all scoffed, but give him his due, it worked, even if the warnings were slightly muffled and Frank and I ended up with black circles around our lips!

The plan was to get out of the area and fast, or as fast as a coal lorry could travel. There was a general feeling of excitement and exhilaration of a job well done. We'd done it, actually fucking done it. It was the climax of months and months of planning. No one knew what to say, and for a moment or two there was an uncomfortable silence, a serious silence.

Each of us was lost in our own thoughts waiting for something to go wrong or listening for the police sirens to wail. As soon as we realised there were no sirens or police following us, I broke the silence and burst into a song, ''Ave a drink, 'ave a drink, 'ave a drink on me.'

All the boys joined in with the chorus: 'Everybody 'ave a drink on me.' We roared with laughter as we trundled our way back to the East End singing at the tops of our voices. To any onlooker walking down the road they may have thought they were on *Candid Camera* or *Beadle's About* witnessing a singing coal lorry; that, or they must have thought they were going slightly cuckoo.

Our euphoria was short-lived when the muffled voice of Frank came down the hoover pipe into my ear warning us of a road-block ahead. I motioned to the others, 'Keep it down boys, it's the Old Bill.'

We froze, not daring to move a muscle. Frank stopped the lorry at the road-block, rolled down his window trying to act normal and asked:

'Problem, mate?'

The copper asked if he'd seen anything suspicious.

'Like what?' he replied. All the time he tried to act polite to avoid any animosity, because that was the last thing we wanted. The copper was cagey, he was giving nothing away. We kept as still as we could, hardly daring to breathe. While one copper kept Frank talking, two others walked around the lorry. We could hear them, sense them, smell them. We looked at each other, all sitting in the back of a coal truck with six cases of money and only a breath away from being caught.

No words were necessary. We were motionless, apart from our eyes looking at each other for reassurance, for support, for something. The coppers prodded and poked at the lorry until they were satisfied nothing was suspicious.

We continued our journey to the East End having made it through the road-blocks, but only just. There we were, five hairy-arsed robbers trapped in the back of a coal truck with exhaust fumes pouring in making the air thick with carbon monoxide. Our eyes were streaming, we were coughing and spluttering, but one look at our spoils made it all worthwhile. The fumes might have stopped us singing, but they didn't stop us grinning.

By the time we got to Albie's flat we looked like five chimney sweeps, but that didn't matter. The only thing that mattered was what was in the cases, or should I say, how much was in the cases. One by one we jemmied them open and emptied the contents on to the floor. There were bundles and bundles of dough, all in £1,000, £2,000 and £5,000 wraps. The stack got higher and higher. Colin ripped the paper wraps off and threw bundles of cash into the air, there was a sea of money across the carpet. Albie took charge while we eagerly counted the notes. There was £87,300 10s.0d. stacked on a threadbare carpet in a council flat in the East End, today's equivalent to nearly £2 million. We didn't look like millionaires but we certainly felt like it. In fact, I started to sing, 'Who wants to be a ...'

All the boys started laughing, and Charlie pleaded, 'No, Roy, don't start singing again, PLEASE.'

We divided the money equally ten ways. Our firm consisted of ten men, and although all ten weren't present, all ten had an equal share. That's the way we ran our firm, the fairest way; our golden rule was share and share alike, whether involved in the job or not. We cut up the money each receiving £8,730.00, leaving one ten bob note on the carpet. If we had followed our golden rule of share and share alike we should have had a bob each, 'a bob a job'. Instead, Albie pressed the orange ten bob note into my hand, winked, and sang ''Ave a drink, 'ave a drink, 'ave a drink on me.' All of us joined in and, at the tops of our voices, sang, 'Everybody 'ave a drink on me.'

I drove all the way home humming that bleeding tune, I couldn't wait to see Carolina, to show her all the money. By the time I reached the front door, I was almost fit to burst. She opened the door with a face like a slapped arse, the baby blues patently obvious, and she hardly drew breath as she fired one question after another at me.

'Where've you been? What have you been doing? Who've you been with?'

I walked passed her without saying a word, the money stuffed inside my shirt. She slammed the door and followed me into the bedroom and stood in the doorway. Her lips sucked into her teeth, her arms folded tight across her chest as she tapped her foot impatiently. With a spiteful look on her face she said, 'Didn't you hear me, I said ...'

I looked at her as I unbuttoned my shirt. I never uttered a word as the money cascaded on to the bed.

'Oooh, Roy ...'

Later that night, I stayed in to watch the television, eager for news on the robbery. On the *Nine O'Clock News* the newsreader announced, 'Bandits' daring raid on security van.' I put down my well-earned drink as I listened carefully to see what they had found out. They knew nothing and I breathed a sigh of relief. Over the next few weeks, I spoilt Carolina, buying her everything she wanted. After the birth of Gary she'd felt quite depressed, it was a woman's thing, something I didn't understand and, to be honest, I didn't want to. But while she was counting all that money on the bed she seemed somewhat brighter, chirpier even, and I swear I saw a little smile appear on her face. There's nothing quite like a big stash of money to make your wife smile again!

Carolina was happy and so were the children, so there was no reason on earth why I couldn't treat myself to a little present in the shape of a bright shiny white Mercedes. I felt like Arthur Daley in the TV series *Minder*, as I meandered around the car showroom in a new cashmere overcoat. The saleswoman was falling over herself to help me choose a car. I toyed with her, keeping her guessing. Was I a time-waster or wasn't I? 'Mmmm ... shall I have the white Merc or the blue Merc?'

The saleswoman tittered just like Barbara Windsor in a *Carry On* film. She flirted openly with me as she said, 'I prefer the white one, sir,' hoping she could persuade me. I smirked and replied, 'White it is then, darling.'

Bang. I had caught her off guard, she'd had me down as a time-waster. She tried to act cool but her eyes gave her away. She stuttered slightly 'Er ... er ... how do you want to pay, sir? Hire purchase or ...'

I puffed out my chest, shrugged my shoulders, stretched my neck, winked and replied, 'Cash, sweetheart. All cash.'

She melted like ice cream in front of me, she was putty in my hands. In reality she must have thought me a flash bastard as she showed me into the small office to do the business. Maybe out of devilment or bravado or just because I was showing off – but God only knows why – I paid £1,012 entirely in £1 notes and one ten shilling note. I knew that ten bob note would come in handy!

10 October 1963 is a day I will never forget. As I left my house on that cold October morning, little did I realise I wouldn't return home for over ten years. I slammed the front door, unaware I was closing it on my home, my wife, my babies and my life.

The day started just like any other. My baby son was only six weeks old and full of colic, his crying had kept me awake most of the night and to make matters worse, my one-year-old daughter was teething. Carolina was exhausted, I tried to do my bit, but gripe water and nappies were just not my thing. I had been wandering around the kitchen since six that morning, comforting my son. I had a terry towelling nappy over my shoulder while patting his back and dodging the drying nappies that were hanging from a makeshift line. There were no such things as tumble dryers or disposable nappies in those days. I couldn't wait to get out of the house; I would rather have faced a court for GBH than two screaming babies, although I love my children dearly. All this domestic stuff had done my head in.

Thinking back on it now, the whole day had had a bad feel about it. I'd arranged to meet Dickie Sullivan in the West End at a pub called The Merry Fiddlers, as he was going to court with me. I drove to the West End in my Merc. Sitting in the traffic that morning I had a gut feeling that something wasn't right. I parked in a side road, and Dickie was waiting in his car. He stuck his head out of the window and shouted, 'Roy, we'll take my car.'

I was puzzled, but without questioning him I jumped into the passenger seat. All the way to the court I had an unnerving feeling something wasn't right, I couldn't quite put my finger on it. We chatted and laughed all the way there but there was something about Dickie that was different. I appeared before the magistrate only to be told the case had been adjourned to the following week.

On the journey home, I was aggravated and was moaning to Dickie about the court being adjourned and what a waste of time it had all been. I should have known something was wrong as Dickie hardly said a word. I noticed he kept looking in his rear-view mirror and seemed very nervous. I knew Dickie had been pulled a few days earlier about the robbery in Longfield, but I wasn't unduly concerned as a number of well-known faces had been pulled, questioned and released.

We approached the side-road where my car was parked, but instead of turning into it Dickie drove straight past.

'Whoah ... stop ... there's my motor.'

Instead of stopping, Dickie drove on.

'Er ... I'll drop you at the end of the road, Roy.'

It was at that point that alarm bells started ringing. Why didn't he just stop the motor? He knew where my car was parked. Why the end of the road? Dickie eventually stopped the car, and he didn't look at me as I got out. I stood on the pavement and watched him disappear out of sight. The road seemed unusually quiet, there was no one about as I walked towards my car. When I reached the corner it reminded me of a ghost town. I looked behind and over my shoulder, there were no other cars parked near mine which was unusual on a busy side-road. I fumbled in my pocket to find my key. No sooner had I put the key in the lock when all hell broke loose. The police appeared like a swarm of bees from nowhere; they scrambled over walls, out of doorways, and appeared like rats from a sewer. Before I knew it, I was face-down eating dirt with a knee in my back and being read my rights.

'Royston Henry Shaw, I am arresting you on suspicion of armed robbery on a security van in Longfield, Kent. You are not obliged to say anything but what you do say will be taken down and used in evidence against you.'

Within days, I and five others appeared before the High Court in Maidstone. Beside me in the dock were Colin and John. Standing next to me was a tall, skinny man. I thought he was a copper until the charges were read out. 'John William Stupple, you are charged with ...'

I whispered out of the corner of my mouth to him, 'Who the fuck are you?' I can honestly say that I'd never seen him before in my life and he certainly wasn't on any armed robbery with me.

Also charged was a young kid who was no older than 21, called William Curbishly. He had also been charged with the same crime, but he hadn't been on the armed robbery either. Both of the men were innocent. I've got no reason to lie and nothing to gain by saying otherwise.

. The hearing lasted six days. They brought in an endless stream of witnesses from a GPO man who said he saw everything from the top of his telegraph pole to the saleswoman from the car showroom who teetered into the court in her high heels. Evidence was mounting against me; I didn't have a hope in hell. I knew I was going away, and I thought eight to ten years at the most. I was the first one to be sentenced.

They brought the Judge in specially for the sentencing. He was a tough old bird, so we knew the sentence would be unusually long. In his summing up, the Judge, Mr Justice Thesiger, said, 'The robbery was carried out quite ruthlessly and over £80,000 is still in the hands of the robbers. I have to deter other people from doing this. Royston Henry Shaw, you will go to prison for 15 years.'

I took a deep breath, it was like a punch in the ribs. Fifteen years. But the Judge hadn't finished yet.

'Shaw, you will also serve another three years for grievous bodily harm, to run consecutively.'

Fifteen, plus three, that's eighteen years. Eighteen fucking years. The bastard had sentenced me to eighteen years' imprisonment.

CHAPTER 7

TEN GRAND TICKET TO RIDE

'My schedule consisted of a 100 sit-ups, 100 press-ups, and I'd use the only thing that was available to me which was my metal-framed bed. I'd lift it over my head 50 times a set, which exercised my shoulder muscles just as well as a dumb-bell, all to be repeated twice a day.'

I SAT ON THE SMALL METAL-FRAMED BED in the police cell, looking at the four grey walls that surrounded me. I read the graffiti left by other prisoners that had been etched into the brickwork, and thought about the Judge's sentence.

He'd said I was to go to prison for 18 years. I heard the words but I didn't understand their meaning. As I sat alone in my cell, my first thoughts were for my children. My daughter, my precious Chatina, was only a year old and to think I had complained only a short while ago about her constant grizzling while teething. It was now I realised I would miss her growing up. Her first steps, first words, seeing her wear that pretty little christening gown I had bought her. Her first day at school and, worst of all, her first boyfriend. What if he took a liberty with her? I wouldn't be there to protect her.

My son would be 18 years old when I was released. Eighteen years. If I said it slowly it didn't seem much, but if you think about it and try to look back over the past 18 years, it's almost impossible to imagine it.

I was 27 years old. I worked out I would be 45 when released. The best years of my life gone in a blink of an eye. Of course, I'd been in prison many times for short spells. It goes with the territory, the hazards of the job, my job – villainy.

The first year of a prison sentence is the hardest. I knew from experience that I could cope, but could my wife?

Carolina was a lovely-looking girl and 18 years was a long time to go without a man. I knew it would be only a matter of time before someone would come sniffing about. It was only human nature and I had seen it a dozen times before with other friends who'd gone away. Anxiously, I asked myself questions. Who would look after her? Who would protect her? Who would look after the kids? Was our marriage strong enough to take it?

What if this? What if that? All unanswerable questions that I could do nothing about. What was I doing to myself? It's like the old saying: 'If you can't do the time, don't commit the crime.' Well, the way I saw it, I had committed the crime, I had the money to prove it, now I had to get on with it and do the time, even if it was 18 long years.

I was sent to Wandsworth Prison in London. In those days, prisons were tough, prisoners were not allowed to talk and a deathly silence hung over the cold, wrought-iron landings. The food was terrible; you were only allowed one egg a year at Easter and your one treat was Christmas Day when it was fish and chips for dinner.

In the Sixties, the police were feared by the younger generation and usually a cuff round the ear would be enough to keep them on the straight and narrow. There weren't so many youngsters in prison then, it was mostly men, hard-nosed criminals, long-termers.

The policy was to use the men as unpaid labour, giving them menial jobs that people on the outside didn't want to or wouldn't do. One such job was sewing mailbags which has since become synonymous with prisons.

It was while I was in the mailbag room laboriously sewing sacks that I found myself sitting next to the infamous Ronnie

Biggs. A few weeks after I was sentenced, he received a 30-year jail term for his part in the Great Train Robbery, even though his role in its organisation was minor. Right from the word go, Biggsy and I hit it off. We had a lot in common; we were both Londoners, both robbers and, unfortunately, both in prison. It was while we were sewing mailbags that he told me about his daring escape plan – ingenious but simple.

'I'm 'aving it away on me toes, Roy. If you want in, it'll cost ya ten long 'uns. Ten grand, that's the price of your freedom.'

I thought long and hard about it. I was facing 18 years inside or a ten grand ticket to ride. I weighed up all the pros and cons (if you'll pardon the pun!) I knew that if I escaped I would need a lot of back-up money. It wasn't only a ten grand ticket, that was just the price to get over the wall; it's what comes once you're over the wall. The price of a forged passport, money for tickets to go abroad, general living expenses, and once people know you're hot, prices go through the roof. But I couldn't dismiss the idea altogether. I needed time to think about it. For the next week, that was all Biggsy and I talked about. He told me everything, all the ins and outs of a duck's arse and more, how he was travelling to Antwerp in the hold of a cargo ship, then on to Paris for a face-lift. His journey was going to be a long one via Sydney, Australia, then Panama, Caracas and finally Rio de Janeiro.

Ronnie Biggs left nothing to chance. If anything, he was over-cautious. He had to be – he was, after all, attempting to escape from one of Her Majesty's big houses.

Shortly after that, I was moved to Parkhurst on the Isle of Wight. I was lying on my bunk when another prisoner came in and said, 'Ronnie Biggs has gone over the wall.'

I smiled to myself. Biggsy must have felt like Steve McQueen in the film *The Great Escape*. Good on him. There have been many times throughout my prison sentence when I've envied Biggsy and wished I'd taken him up on his offer.

When you're alone in your cell at night your mind wanders, that was my escape. I would journey to better places and far-off shores with white talcum powder beaches and a bronzed beauty beside me sipping a pina colada. If only. I was pleased for him and I'm glad he has managed to elude the Metropolitan Police force for over 34 years. I must take my hat off to the man. I could never have stayed away from Blighty for so long. It's not just friends and family I'd miss, a rainy day or a nice cup of tea, it's a combination of all of those things, in fact it's almost indefinable.

As I finish writing this book in December 1998, I will be flying out to Rio de Janeiro to see my old mate Biggsy. I arrive in Rio on Christmas Day and my escape to beaches, babes and pina coladas is no longer a dream. There might have been a slight delay of 34 years but I got there in the end.

Prison life can, if you let it, lead to a certain deterioration of your ability to do things for yourself. The very detailed planning of every minute of your day can either destroy you or make you stronger. You have to be tough to survive long spells of confinement.

When you're in prison you've got nothing to think about, nothing to occupy your mind, you don't even have to think about where your next meal is coming from. You can't go anywhere, you haven't got a bus or train to catch. The main event of the month is a visit for two precious hours, and the worse thing any visitor can be is late.

Carolina made the long journey from Essex to Portsmouth, then over on the ferry to the Isle of Wight as often as she could, but with two small babies it wasn't easy. Often she was late for a visit, and that wound me up. Every second with her was precious. She used all the excuses under the sun: 'There was a lot of traffic on the road ... the ferry was late ... blah, blah, blah ...'

All we had was two hours a month, and I didn't want to miss a minute, let alone half an hour listening to her tearful excuses and then spend the next half-hour arguing the toss. After a year inside, the cracks in our marriage were beginning to show. But instead of discussing it with her, I got totally fucked off. If I had thought about it logically, I would have realised that a different approach was needed, but prison doesn't teach you to be logical. Maybe I was being paranoid, but I really didn't think she wanted to visit me any more. I didn't want to lose her, but our marriage was on a road to nowhere.

In retrospect, those first years away I lived my life through Carolina, expecting her to do all the things I was unable to do because I was locked up. I didn't give enough thought to her being alone in the outside world with the kids, Chatina and Gary. It must have been tough, but I was young and selfish. I never wondered how she was going to feed them, clothe them, as well as coming to visit me every month. That's without writing daily, and me ordering her to do this or do that, and then when she did get to see me once a month all I did was give out to her. I realise now it was no life for Carolina being a prisoner's wife.

It's assumed that it's glamorous being married to a gangster – all fur coat and no knickers – but the reality is spending all day travelling to a prison in the middle of nowhere and standing outside in the rain waiting to have the humiliation of being searched, only to have a moany old bastard barking at you for two hours. There's more to life than that.

If you marry a villain, then you know the score, but I felt terrible for Carolina. I missed her when I was banged up. I've always found the soppy stuff hard to express, but Carolina seemed to understand that, and for the first time I felt that someone loved me just as I was. Nothing seemed to put her off; she took it all in her stride, and her love meant the world to me.

But our marriage was starting to fall apart at the seams and I realised it would be only a matter of time before I got the big heave-ho, the elbow, the gooner, the 'Dear John' – whatever you want to call it. I knew it was coming, it was just a matter of time.

*   *   *

In Parkhurst, mail was distributed every Tuesday and Friday. I always started to get anxious the night before letter day and would pace around my cell from the early hours, worried that I would receive the 'Dear John'. By the time the screw unlocked my cell, I was ready to explode, my hands were sweating, I had been through every possible scenario in my mind. If there wasn't a letter, I could cope with that by assuming Carolina had missed the post, but if there was a letter was it the one I had dreaded? No sooner had the lock in my cell clicked, I'd holler at the screw, 'WHERE'S MY LETTER? WHERE'S MY LETTER?'

I had been kidding myself all along when I thought I could cope if there was no letter for me. I would make the screws go through the bundles twice, checking and double checking. If there was a letter I would sit on my bed staring at the envelope, hoping and praying it was an 'I love you and I miss you', and not the dreaded alternative. If, on the other hand, there wasn't one, I would be like a bear with a sore head, nothing and no one could pacify me.

Every Tuesday and Friday was the same. I would wind myself up into such a frenzy, and take it out on anyone who got near me. That's exactly what happened to my old mate Albert Rainbird when he arrived at Parkhurst on a six month lay-down.

Rainbird had been a mate of mine for years, having worked together on numerous occasions. When I say 'work' I mean armed robberies, and he was even involved in the beigel fiasco and we'd served time together. I'm loath to say I considered him a close friend. In the past, we'd always looked out for each other. Rainbird loved a row, but more so, he loved seeing me have a row. Metaphorically speaking, he'd load the gun and I would be the one to fire it.

I'd heard through the grapevine that Rainbird had turned bad, that he was a wrong 'un. It was double bad because I had considered him a friend. When I heard he was a grass, at first I couldn't believe it. How could I have got him so wrong? It really knocked me back. I knew for a fact he had started putting young girls on the game, and living off their immoral earnings. In my book, that made him a no-good pimp. To make matters worse, he'd grassed on one of the firm – one of our old mates who we used to do jobs with. In short, he turned out to be a right old mongrel.

When Rainbird arrived at Parkhurst, I decided that his number was up, he had played his games for long enough, I was going to hurt him, and hurt him bad. I wanted him to look in the mirror every morning with something to remember me by. To hurt someone you need a blade or a piece of glass, and the only glass available was my hair cream bottle. Things had been getting on top of me – I was fed up, cheesed off, and to top it all Carolina hadn't written and I wasn't due a visit for two weeks. I didn't need excuses to cut Rainbird, but he had caught me at a particularly low ebb. I was like a seething volcano ready to erupt at any moment.

I smashed the bottle and sharpened the glass on the stone window sill until it was as sharp as a razor. I slipped my makeshift knife into my pocket and went out into the exercise yard. I sunk my hands deep into the pockets of my donkey jacket and wandered around the exercise yard looking for Rainbird until I spotted him. I couldn't take my eyes off of him. He was laughing and chatting with a screw, unaware of what I was about to do to him. Talking to a screw? Nobody does that, not unless they are a no-good grass.

There was plenty of activity in the exercise yard and lots of eyes and ears. I had to pick my moment, I didn't want to get caught – and go to prison! Ha bloody ha. The whistle blew signalling the end of the recreation period, and the prisoners filed back on to the wing. I made my way through the line of men until I was standing next to Rainbird. I was breathing heavily as I watched him take his final drag from a cigarette, drop it on to the ground and grind his foot on it to extinguish it.

Now was my chance. I grabbed the unsuspecting Rainbird by the hair forcing his head back. He had a look of shock and disbelief on his face as I dragged my makeshift blade across his throat. It only took a second. He let out a blood-curdling scream which alerted the guards. He was rasping for breath, terror-stricken, clutching his neck with both hands. In a split second, he tried to call for help but there were no words, he tried to gasp for breath but there was no air, and he tried to stop the blood gushing from his neck but there was no way. His eyes bulged, he had a look of fear and panic on his face as I screamed at him, 'TAKE A GOOD LOOK AT MY FACE, RAINBIRD, THIS IS THE LAST FACE YOU'LL SEE ON EARTH,' then I punched him and down he went.

The alarm rang out, whistles blew and we were ushered on to the wing. Rainbird was carted off to hospital and was on the danger list for a while. I didn't give a fuck if I'd killed him or not. The doctors saved his life but only just. In my opinion, he wasn't worth saving; he was a dirty mongrel, a throw-back, the runt of the litter and, in a dog-eat-dog world, the runt of the litter is drowned at birth.

The daily grind of prison is dull, boring and predictable and if you don't find things to occupy your mind it can be your downfall. In 1965, while I was away, the suicide rate was high, until new legislation was introduced in the early Seventies giving prisoners the opportunity for further education. That's why there are so many aspiring poets, artists and scholars in prison nowadays. Well, I'm no artist, poet or scholar but on the other hand I wasn't prepared to bow down to anyone. I did the only thing I knew how to do – training and fighting.

I'd spend hour after hour training in my cell. My daily fitness routine was vigorous, and I'd set my standards high pushing myself to the limit. My schedule consisted of a 100 sit-ups, 100 press-ups, and I'd use the only thing that was available to me which was my metal-framed bed. I'd lift it over my head 50 times a set, which exercised my shoulder muscles just as well as a dumb-bell, all to be repeated twice a day.

At that point in my sentence, the Governor and the screws were glad I was keeping myself occupied because I had become so violent I was a liability. Making me conform to their petty rules and regulations was beyond them.

When I was in my cell training I was out of the way, and all the time I was occupied I was less likely to do any damage to anyone or anything. If I was happy, they were happy.

On a rare occasion, something broke the routine and lightened the mood on the wing. One particular officer was a cruel bastard, and must have been pensioned off from either the police force or the Army. Usually, all the throw-backs from the armed forces and the like end up as prisoner officers.

For whatever reason, they leave their chosen profession and enter the prison service. It's usually with a vindinctive nature, or a chip on their shoulder. This officer was a prime example. He had an ability to see a weakness in a person and use it to his own advantage, exposing their vulnerability for all and sundry to see. For months, I witnessed him picking on a young kid, a greenhorn. He wasn't a hard-nosed criminal, just a misguided, inexperienced, gullible youth, perhaps a little slow for his age. You know the sort – a loner who lives with his elderly mum. Take him out of that environment and throw him into the harsh reality of prison life and he'll fold, especially when continually picked on. I felt sorry for him but I couldn't fight everyone's battles or wipe everyone's snotty nose. The young kid had to do one of two things; either go under or kick back. The officer knew the kid couldn't take it and teased him relentlessly, calling him a mummy's boy. Perhaps the boy could take the physical but not the mental abuse. Often I would pass him on the landing, where he'd be sporting a black eye, and at night I'd often hear him crying in his cell. He never said anything to anyone, just kept himself to himself. None of the other cons spoke about it, but we all witnessed from afar what was going on.

The final straw came when, for two whole days, The officer never left the kid alone. He was on his back relentlessly, and it was blatantly obvious that the boy had reached the end of his tether. He had been pushed over the edge and couldn't take any more. He took an overdose of laxatives.

Throughout the night he was on his chamber pot, and by morning it was full to the brim. I watched the kid come out of his cell, his glazed expression giving nothing away as he slowly walked along the landing holding his pot full of shit towards a group of officers who were standing having their early morning chin wag. To this day, I'm still not sure how many other prisoners on the landing had been secretly, in their own way, keeping an eye on the kid or maybe it was just his entire demeanour, but everyone stopped what they were doing and watched. All eyes were on the kid.

The youngster got to the end of the landing and Pugh spotted him. The kid's face was expressionless as he took the makeshift lid off the pot and threw its entire contents over the screws. He aimed well. Most of the foul smelling muck went over his tormentor who was in the process of shouting a warning because his mouth was wide open. For a moment, he stood frozen to the spot, completely helpless as a deluge of greeny, yellow, brownish gunge dribbled from his mouth. The whole landing cheered. From that day on he became known as 'Stinky Poo', a nickname that stuck with him for years.

These occasional funny moments were few and far between. Prison, on the whole, is one huge cesspit and something I would never recommend to anyone. It's not big and it's not clever to go to prison, it's a complete and utter waste of human life. If you just step back for a moment and ask yourself – Just what is prison? In my experience, it's a huge holding tank into which all the men whom society can no longer tolerate are dumped. All the murderers, the rapists, the armed robbers, the thieves, the cut-throats, are contained in one big building. On top of that, you deny these men their fundamental rights as human beings. To deny them their liberty is one thing, but to strip away their dignity by denying them even the right to use a toilet is another. They are thrust head-first into a male-dominated world, which is like a melting pot of evil that evokes riots over the slightest thing. In any pack of animals, there is only one dominant male, and in any family, the male is usually the dominant one. The point is all these dominant males are taken away from their packs and confined together for months and years. There's no getting away from it, it's a recipe for disaster.

Each man has to deal with his own problems, whatever they may be – money problems, drug problems, sexual problems, it all increases the tension. And add to that a sprinkling of madness from a few, and what have you got? A dangerous, unpredictable, violent house on the hill with a disaster waiting to happen. Believe me, prison is a very, very dangerous place, containing men with nothing to lose but a lot to prove.

Everyone has their own cross to bear. Mine was my suspicious mind because by this time I had serious thoughts about my wife's fidelity and I was finding it increasingly difficult to control my violent rages that bordered on insanity. Looking back on it now, I think the angels must have given me a light dusting of madness, too.

The strength I had built up with the constant training in my cell over a period of two years, combined with my bad temper, can be likened to the combination of nitro-glycerine and a detonator. Separately they are safe, but put them together and it's dynamite. If that wasn't dangerous enough, add a game of Sunday afternoon football between prisoners and screws and it forms a chemical compound more dangerous than the atom bomb!

The prisoners had a good football team, including a professional football player called Micky Machin who played for West Ham United – when he was out, of course! Then there was Alfie Hutchinson. I liked him because he was up-front, said what he had to say and damned the rest. We had a strong team, no one ever beat us.

The Principal Officer tried. He was always the football referee, and was obviously biased against us. It was the usual Sunday afternoon grudge match and with two minutes left before half time, I scored a goal, but it was disallowed which made me cop the needle with the PO referee. He blew his whistle, turned his back on me and walked away leaving me fuming. I had scored fair and square, but he treated me with total contempt.

I could have exploded with the frustration and injustice of it all, and without even thinking about it, I picked up half a house brick from the side of the pitch and threw it.

Talk about players taking a dive! Anyone would think he'd been shot by a cannon. He rolled on the ground clutching his shoulder screaming in agony. He could have won an Oscar for his performance. I didn't know what all the fuss was about. Alf ran towards me shaking his head in disbelief.

'Fuck me, Roy, you've got to sort your temper out. It's only a game.'

The game finished early and we were taken back on to the wing where we were all sent back to work. Alf worked in the Officers' Mess and would often steal tea cakes and smuggle them out to share among us. Later that evening, Alf came into my cell with his pockets full of little snacks and delights. Alf wasn't one to mince his words and said what he had to say.

'I've heard talk in the Officers' Mess that you're being watched,' he said. 'They can't handle you, they're shit scared of you, Roy.'

He went on to tell me about a psychiatric unit called Grendon Underwood. He made it sound great and said I would even be allowed conjugal rights once a month. Mmm ... I liked the sound of that. Conjugal visits! Alf must have read my mind because he laughed and nodded. I wanted to keep my marriage together and at that time I was prepared to try anything, even Grendon Underwood. In my poor deluded mind, I thought that was the answer to all my problems.

Within days, I was sitting in the psychiatrist's office. It must have been the quickest appointment anyone had ever got. To be honest, I think Parkhurst couldn't wait to get rid of me and was just passing the buck. The psychiatrist dotted the i's and crossed the t's – it was as simple as that to be certified insane.

Some years later, I saw the film *One Flew Over the Cuckoo's Nest* starring Jack Nicholson. As I was escorted through the secure gates at Grendon Underwood hospital years earlier, I played the main character to a tee. I was nonchalant and cocky and didn't think there was anything wrong with me at all, I was just there for my monthly conjugal visits.

As in the film, we also used to have group therapy sessions with approximately 30 men sitting in a circle talking about their problems. For the first few weeks I wouldn't co-operate, I didn't want to bare my soul to complete strangers. I didn't share my innermost thoughts and feelings with my wife let alone a bunch of nutters. After a few weeks on the ward, there are only so many card games you can play, so just to break the monotony I agreed to sit in just to see what was going on.

The motley group took their usual seats. The male doctor was wet behind the ears and fresh out of university, a typical left-wing hippie with new-wave ideas, wearing a hand-knitted tank top. He'd been on all the 'Ban the Bomb' marches and wore the badge to prove it. He asked if anyone wanted to get anything off their chest.

A patient sitting opposite me put his hand up. I looked at the man. He wasn't the sort of person you'd expect to find in a nut house, he had an air of respectability about him. At first he seemed reluctant to speak about his problems but with a little coaxing from the doctor his lurid story started to unfold. He explained that he wanted to unburden himself and hopefully get help. I studied him carefully as he began to speak.

'It all started a few months ago when I became obsessed with a dog. I think I fell in love with her.'

My jaw dropped open. In love with a fucking dog?

'Please continue, Derick,' the doctor urged.

I sat in total silence and listened as Derick went into graphic detail of how he had full sex with this poor dog. Ever since I was a kid and had been evacuated to Chippenham, I have adored dogs. They really are man's best friend, they are faithful to their master no matter what. When I heard the disgusting things that the twisted pervert had put that poor animal through, I couldn't believe what I was hearing. I suppressed my instinct to get up and hurt him. Instead, I interrupted the group by putting my hand up. The doctor asked:

'You have a question, Roy?'

'Mmm ... I'd just like to ask Derick what breed of dog it was?'

Everybody looked at each other and smirked. I'm sure I saw tears in Derick's eyes as he answered, 'Alsatian, Roy, she was an Alsatian.'

'Good-looking dog, was it?' I said sarcastically.

The doctor looked at me, then at Derick. He may well have been used to dealing with perverts, listening to their debauched evil fantasies, but I wasn't. Sensing this, he stood up, feebly attempting to diffuse a volatile situation, but it was too late – I already had Derick by the throat.

I never returned to the group therapy session again. It was then I realised Grendon Underwood was not the sort of place I wanted to be associated with. It was full of nonce cases. In prison, nonces are attacked regularly. If I'd hurt every nonce I came across in Grendon, I would have been throwing punches 24 hours a day. I had to get out of there at whatever cost.

Carolina was due to visit me the following Thursday morning. We hadn't been getting on well at all. I'd been in prison for two years and the strain was taking its toll on us both. I'd been looking forward to seeing her, that's all I had been thinking about for days, I'd even managed to buy her some flowers. I wanted to make our marriage work, and really hoped she felt the same way. I tried to read between the lines in her letters but they gave nothing away.

Keeping our marriage alive was what I wanted more than anything. I'd been gearing up for this day and wanted things to be right, I wanted it so much it hurt. It was one of those situations which I'm sure most people have experienced at one time or another, when you are really excited about seeing someone and look forward to it so much, but from the outset something goes wrong. That's just what happened to me on that fated Thursday morning with Carolina.

I was up early humming to myself as I washed and shaved. I even borrowed a splash of cologne, I wanted to look my best. I looked at Carolina's bouquet of flowers on my bed, picked them up and inhaled their fragrant perfume. I thought she'd love them. All night, I'd been thinking about what I was going to say to her; I just wanted to put things right between us. After all, it doesn't matter who says sorry, as long as someone does. Today, I decided I was going to be the one to apologise. I was going to kiss and make up. Every time I thought of Carolina my belly flipped over and a warm feeling of anticipation swept over me.

I was informed that Carolina was waiting in the hall. Heart pounding, I picked up the flowers and made my way through to see her. She looked gorgeous, absolutely stunning. I looked her up and down. On one hand I was so proud of her, but on the other I noticed her blouse was a bit low-cut, and her make-up was a bit over the top. She looked lovely, but people were looking at her. Added to that she wore red nail varnish, tarty red nail varnish, which she knew I didn't like. If I'd told her once I'd told her a dozen times that only tarts wore red nail varnish. So instead of saying what I wanted to say, how pleased I was to see her and how beautiful she looked, I got it all wrong as usual. As the words were tumbling out, I wished I could take them back, but it was too late, Carolina was already in tears.

I tried to pacify her and calm her down, I gave her the flowers and put my arm around her but she was having none of it; she pushed me away and threw the flowers in my face. It had all gone wrong. I didn't know what to say. I had said enough anyway, I was only digging a hole for myself so I turned on my heels and went back to the ward, disappointed and angry. I was angry with the screws, angry with Carolina but, most of all, angry with myself. I felt worthless. I loved her, but it seemed I could only push her away. My male pride and arrogance wouldn't allow me to be wrong. I wanted to blame everybody but myself and lashed out in the only way I knew how.

I let out an almighty cry of frustration as I picked up my bed and threw it across my cell. The other patients ran for their lives. I closed my eyes tight as my tormented mind took me on a downward spiral to the depths of despair. My head was pounding, I felt the veins in my neck stand out, my eyes bulged as I clenched my fist and pummelled my forehead again and again.

I wanted to hurt myself as I had hurt Carolina. Everything had gone dreadfully wrong. I lost control. I finally cracked. I suppose it was at that point I realised my marriage was over. I wanted to run after her to tell her I was sorry, to ask her to forgive me, but I couldn't, I was locked in. I had to get out, I had to see her, and I knew that once she'd left the hospital, she would be gone for good and I'd never see her again.

Grendon Underwood sent in their finest foot soldiers to restrain me. I had the strength of ten men as I tore the butler sink from the wall, bursting the pipes, but even the icy spray of cold water wouldn't cool my rage. I tugged at the metal support until it came away in my hand, and I stood alone in the ward with the only friends I knew – my iron cosh and my pride. It was them and me.

All my life I have had to fight, in the playground with the bullies, in the Army with the Sergeants, in the Borstal with the 'daddies', and now with the male nurses in the nut house. Well, I'll fight until I die.

'Come on, you bastards, I'll kill every last one of ya.'

I fought for my life and bashed every screw who came within my reach. With every swing of the iron cosh I could see a bully fall in front of me, a Sergeant fall in front of me, a 'daddy' fall in front of me. I continued lashing out until I dropped to my knees exhausted.

What happened next is unclear, in fact, the following week was just a blur. I don't know if I was injected with drugs, fell unconscious or what.

The next thing I remember was sitting in the doctor's office. I listened to him in a daze and never uttered a word as he told me I could no longer stay in the hospital. I had become too uncontrollable for prison and too violent for Grendon, so there was only one place left for me to go – Broadmoor.

CHAPTER 8

ONE FLEW OVER ...

'I pulled the hammer back on the gun and aimed it at Malone's head. My mate panicked. At the time, I thought he feared I'd kill Malone, but it wasn't that at all. He pushed my arm towards the ceiling just as the gun fired ...'

FINALLY, I LANDED IN THE NEST. The cuckoo nest. Call it what you want – the funny farm, the nut house, the loony bin – they are all derogatory terms for Broadmoor Hospital for the Criminally Insane. It was inevitable that I would end up in a nut house. Since the age of ten I've been unable to control my temper. I remember vividly that first time I lost control and experienced the adrenalin rush, in the playground with the bullies. It's a feeling I'll never forget; the surge of power is so strong when I lose my temper there is no going back. It's just pure undiluted adrenalin, the brain's most primitive and powerful protector. It heightens awareness and affects all your senses, you don't feel pain and it increases your strength ten-fold. When I experience the 'rush' as I call it, I'm like a man possessed. There is no talking to me and no reasoning. After all, you can't reason with a madman. Doctors said I was unpredictable, uncontrollable, and worse still, unjustifiably violent. I admit I have no conscience, nor pity. If that makes me mad then I'm barking.

Since the dark ages, lunatic asylums have been shrouded in a cloak of secrecy. The word asylum conjures up images of madness that can hit a raw nerve in us all. Deny it if you like, but every human being has the ability to go crazy.

Often, we use the phrase 'I'm going mad' lightly, but the reality is we are all capable of being driven over the edge. That's the reason why madness frightens us all, because we all dread walking in those shoes. Perhaps we should bear in mind the phrase: 'There, but for the grace of God, go I.'

The word 'bedlam' means an asylum for lunatics, and the words lunatic asylum is now an offensive term. Right up until the end of the Second World War, from royalty to the ordinary man in the street, having a mad relative was socially unacceptable, an embarrassment, and totally taboo. It wasn't that many years ago that some poor sods who were perhaps slow, wayward, deemed uncontrollable or had committed some minor misdemeanour were committed to a mental institution.

For example, Billy Giles was sent to Broadmoor in 1886 for setting fire to a haystack. He was never released and died in 1962 after spending 76 years inside. Now that's what you call life imprisonment. This wasn't a one-off; many patients have been in asylums for 30 years or more, often for minor crimes like petty thieving, or being pregnant out of wedlock. Even an unwanted wife was locked up and the key was thrown away. Once committed, the years rolled by and these poor unfortunate souls were forgotten.

Before I start telling you about my horrifying experiences in Broadmoor, let me give you a little bit of an insight into the background of the country's most daunting and mysterious lunatic asylum.

Broadmoor Hospital is 35 miles from London and was the first state institution for the insane. It was built in 1856 and, strangely enough, by convicts. Even after the first patients arrived in 1863, the convicts carried on working within the walls for another couple of years.

The hospital was named Broadmoor simply because it was to

be built on a broad moor in Crowthorne, Berkshire. The architect was Sir Joshua Jebb, who had also designed Pentonville Prison. Prisons and institutions were his speciality, although beauty and design certainly weren't. Broadmoor is a hideous place.

If Jebb designed the place to be intimidating then he succeeded. The hospital is totally self-contained and self-sufficient; in reality, it needs little or no contact with the outside world. The hospital has its own water supply and sewage plant, kitchens, gardens, a small farm and workshops for tailoring, carpentry and metal work. There is even a cemetery and the coffins for those who die are made by patients in the carpenter's shop. In the old cemetery, 1,445 inmates lie buried under freshly mowed grass, forever confined within the walls of Broadmoor. There are no headstones, or even a name saying who they were, just a number etched into a rusty plaque. Throughout their lives, inmates were known only by a number, and in death, nothing had changed.

Years ago, patients weren't offered any kindness or therapy, just shackled and caged and treated like animals, probably rather worse, and their fundamental basic human rights were denied.

Strait-jackets and padded cells were widely used until the 1920s and the arrival of Superintendent Dr Sullivan, who was the first man in the history of the hospital to care about the patients' welfare. He started experimenting with therapy and drugs, which, in those days, were in their infancy. It was a case of trial and error, the blind leading the blind. Doctors had no idea what effect the drugs would have on the patients, whether good or bad. Nobody cared and nobody witnessed the deterioration in the patients because the moment you were locked up, all contact from the outside world was lost, except by letter. Visiting was introduced by Dr Foulerton who replaced Dr Sullivan in 1926, when relatives were allowed to see patients one Sunday every month. But such was the stigma at that time, nobody admitted to having a relative locked in Broadmoor.

Patients were not treated with any humanity whatsoever, with even the simple function of shaving being denied them until as recently as 1944. Razors were forbidden, so all patients had long beards. This unfortunately is the vision we all have of mental asylums, me included. As the massive wooden gates swept shut behind me, I, too, had this vision of lost souls with a vacant look in their eyes and beards to their waists wandering aimlessly. Nothing could have prepared me for what was in store behind the sinister orange brick walls of Broadmoor Hospital for the Criminally Insane.

It was a cold, grey November day in 1965 when I arrived on the doorstep of Broadmoor. The gates swept shut behind me, then there was nothing. It was like entering another world, somewhere I had never been before. The walls were like big arms that totally engulfed me, almost with a false sense of security. I've been in nut houses in Germany and in Grendon Underwood, but none matched the unique feeling I felt as the gates closed behind me at Broadmoor.

The first thing I noticed was the eerie silence. I don't know what I'd expected, but it wasn't the silence. It was a weird experience and only with hindsight can I begin to analyse it. I can liken it to the gardens in a country house where you'd expect to see people, but the place was deserted, as if in a dream. I was escorted through the grounds to the admission block where it was bedlam. I'd gone from one extreme to the other. While the grounds were calm and tranquil, the wards were mayhem, full of nutters and crackpots walking up and down the corridors mumbling to themselves. It was exactly how I'd imagined it, and all that was missing was the long beards.

On the reception wing, I was assessed by an endless team of doctors and nurses. I suppose they wanted to label me 'schizophrenic', 'psychopath', 'demented' or whatever. Once they had established what illness I was suffering from only then could I be given the appropriate medication. I didn't think there was anything wrong with me mentally, and as long as inmates didn't cross me I was just fine and fucking dandy.

The biggest problem on the ward was boredom. After breakfast, there wasn't much to do until lunch. I wasn't really one for socialising, I didn't want to sit playing cards with all the nutters, and I certainly wasn't participating in the group therapy sessions – I'd had enough of that in Grendon. Thank you very much, woof-bloody-woof.

I chose my friends carefully inside prison and out. When I wandered into the recreation room for a game of snooker, there was already a young patient playing. I sat down in a blue leatherette chair; you know the sort – like the ones you find in a geriatric ward, and no matter how hard you try you just can't get comfortable. I watched the patient lean across the table and pot a ball. He put the cue on his shoulder as he walked around the table to get the next angle, then potted another ball, then another.

'Nice shot, mate.' I said. It broke the ice between us. For the next hour, I watched him pot all the balls on the table. We laughed and chatted, and could have been in any snooker hall in any town, in any city – but we weren't. I asked him why he was in Broadmoor.

He rolled his eyes towards heaven. 'Tsk, tsk,' he replied, and with a sharp intake of breath said, 'Don't ask. There's fuck-all wrong with me.'

He continued wandering around the table eyeing up the shots, seeming normal enough. I even felt sorry for him, poor bugger – until, that is, I asked him if he fancied a game of snooker.

'I can't,' he said. 'I'm already playing with me mate,' and pointed to a wide open space next to him. I frowned, looked at the patient, then into thin air. Again, I looked at the patient. 'What fucking mate?' I asked. He started to get agitated and raised his voice.

'Who I've been fucking playing with all this time, whose just whooped the arse off me. That's who.'

I was speechless. That was it. He went off at a tangent, cursing and rowing with the invisible man. I shook my head in disbelief and walked out of the snooker room, sniggering. All I could hear in the distance was the nutter shouting at his mate, 'I'll win the next one, you wait and see ...' Just another day in the loony bin.

I stayed in the admission block for three months, while the

doctors did every test possible. In their humble opinion, they concluded I was a psychopath and I would mellow with age. Hmmm. I could have told them that myself and not wasted the tax-payers' money. Eventually, I was moved on to Block 7 into a single cell measuring 14ft by 8ft. It was very basic but comfortable. For a bed there was a wooden base with a mattress on top. There was a small, heavily barred window with shutters which could be closed and locked if you misbehaved making the cell completely dark. Unlike prison, we were allowed to have our own carpet, curtains and bedding, and there was no prison-issue clothing, we were allowed to wear our own.

I settled down well in Broadmoor and even got a job outside as a brick layer. I didn't mind that, plenty of fresh air and exercise could only do me good. Perhaps I'm making Broadmoor sound like a holiday camp; in lots of ways, it's easier than prison, but only in some.

It's true you can wear your own clothing, the food is better, you can have more visits, and in general it's a less stressful environment. But in order to maintain the air of tranquillity in a place that houses unpredictable violent men with no future and nothing to lose, there has to be a threat or a deterrent and, believe me, the deterrent in Broadmoor is your worst nightmare doubled – no, trebled. There are several ways to control unruly patients, who, in most cases, have twice their normal strength. In order to get control, something has to be done and quickly. Staff in Broadmoor are highly trained to do just that – to bring a patient to their knees in seconds. There is the obvious way of restraining a man with a strait-jacket, and being shackled and fettered, but to manhandle them into the restraints reasonable force has to be applied and the staff in Broadmoor are experts.

The first time I saw it done was in the reception ward. A patient was ranting and raving. He picked up a chair and was screaming abuse, frothing at the mouth threatening patients and staff. He was totally uncontrollable. I watched a male officer slip behind him, put his arm around his neck and squeeze. In a moment it was all over, down he went as if hypnotised.

The staff are taught the exact amount of pressure to apply; not enough and the patient goes berserk, too much and the patient dies. Some patients would argue that they would rather die than spend the rest of their days in Broadmoor. That's just what happened in the case of a young man I met while I was there.

Billy Doyle was a tough guy, and tough guys are not easily pushed around. He wasn't a nutter, just a man with a bad temper. Like me, he'd also had been through the rigours of Borstal, prison, and had inevitably ended up in Broadmoor. I liked Billy. He was an unassuming man who didn't give a fuck about anyone. He'd done his time in Broadmoor and was due to be released, but no patient is ever released back into the community directly from Broadmoor. You either have to return to prison or go to a county hospital and then home. It's like a stepping stone to ease you back into society. You see, in Broadmoor you're very closeted, all the stresses and strains of the outside world are taken away. Your letters are vetted, your visitors are vetted, you don't have to worry about keeping a roof over your head or have any bills to pay, and to go from a stress-free environment to the harsh world of reality has to be done gradually.

Billy Doyle had served his time and was on his way home via a county hospital. Within weeks, the stresses of the outside world were too much for him. I don't know the whys or wherefores, but Billy killed a nurse and was returned to Broadmoor indefinitely.

He arrived on my wing subdued and quiet. He sat alone most of the time, deep in his own thoughts. I didn't say anything to him, there was really nothing to say. It was just another day on the ward, and as usual nothing much was happening. I was sitting reading the newspaper when Billy sat down beside me.

'All right, Roy?' he asked. I looked at Billy, who hadn't spoken to anyone in weeks.

'Yeah, I'm OK,' I answered.

Billy's face looked drawn and tired, his movements seemed sluggish. For a moment or two, there was an uncomfortable silence, neither of us knew what to say. Billy leaned over and said softly in my ear, 'Roy, I want to ask you a favour.'

I put my newspaper down and asked what sort of favour.

Billy Doyle's face was expressionless. His eyes divulged nothing as he whispered. 'Will you kill me, Roy?'

I couldn't believe what I was hearing and told him to shut up. I felt sorry for him and I knew what he was thinking – that he would never be released. If I thought for one minute I would never be released and would have to spend the rest of my days in a lunatic asylum, I, too, would probably be asking the same favour. There was no simple answer.

I tried to dissuade him, and to give him some hope. I said all the time you have breath in your body there is a chance of freedom. He didn't answer me, he just shrugged his shoulders and walked away. I went back to reading my newspaper and didn't give the incident any more thought until the alarm was sounded an hour later. There was a commotion in the washrooms, and Billy Doyle was brought out of the toilets in a body bag. His wish had been granted by another patient on our ward. He strangled Billy for what? Nothing, but just because he'd asked him. Broadmoor is a hopeless place full of despair with hopeless people killing time and each other. As far as I know, he is still killing time in Broadmoor.

My marriage to Carolina was hanging by a thread, it was all but over. She had become more distant, finding silly excuses not to visit me. Her letters no longer came directly to me, instead they went via Dr McGrath. I felt everybody knew something that I didn't. Call it a gut feeling, but I knew something was wrong, and this time I wasn't being paranoid.

I'd been waiting all week for a letter from Carolina but it never arrived. When I enquired, the staff nurse seemed reluctant to answer and evaded the question by saying that Dr McGrath wanted to see me in his office. As soon as the doctor told me to sit down, I knew it could only be one of two things. One, I was dying of cancer and had six months to live; or two, it was a 'Dear John'. It had to be bad news because three officers stood between me and the doctor. I noticed the doctor had my letter from Carolina in his hand. I'm no psychologist but his body language indicated that he was about to tell me a lie. He cleared his throat, fidgeted about in his seat, fiddled with his glasses, ummed and ahhed, and took a deep breath.

'It's your wife, Roy.'

I breathed a sigh of relief. 'Phew ... at least it's not cancer.'

Dr McGrath continued, obviously uncomfortable with the flimsy story he was telling. 'Your wife was having a little trouble with her waterworks.'

The doctor looked at my puzzled face as I mouthed the words, 'Waterworks ...?'

'Taps, Roy, I mean taps.'

I sat in total silence as he whittered on about how the plumber's wife caught her husband and my wife together.

I saw through his veiled attempt to soften the blow but it didn't come as any great surprise to me that Carolina had somebody else. From the moment I was sentenced, she said she was going to wait for me, but talk is cheap and good intentions are two-a-penny.

A few days later, a private visit was arranged for me and my wife to thrash out our problems, one way or another. Give Carolina her due, she had enough courage to tell me face to face. She was coming to see me to explain, but to say what? I'm sorry? Goodbye? Whatever she had to say, it was nothing I wanted to hear.

The nurses expected trouble. Six officers stayed in the little room with us. Carolina never looked at me as she cried. She twiddled and fiddled with her hankie as she explained how she had met another fella, and how he was living with her. To top it all, his wife had written to Broadmoor, in particular to me, to tell me what was going on, but the doctor had intercepted the letter. It seems I was the last to know.

I was man enough to take it on the chin. I wasn't about to let Carolina or the screws see me cry. I looked at her tear-stained face and only remembered the good times. Our first meeting, her perfume – the pungent fragrance of violets that made me so giddy – our wonderful wedding, and her squeals of delight when she counted my ill-gotten gains. She was leaving me, taking away my children. The authorities had taken away my liberty, but no one can take away my memories. I stood up. I wanted to plead with her to change her mind but I had to be strong and pretend I didn't care.

Over the next few weeks I found it difficult to cope. The thought of that man with my wife was driving me nuts. I went through every scenario in my mind, again and again. He wasn't only living in my house with my wife, sleeping in my bed, he was sitting on my sofa with my daughter on his knee. The very thought of it made me sick to my stomach. It was driving me to distraction. I didn't speak to anyone, I couldn't eat anything, in fact I didn't want to leave my cell. An endless team of psychiatrists came to see me, but I just told them to fuck off. There was no pill I could take, or sufficient therapy to change the circumstances, and I certainly didn't want to speak to any namby-pamby, wet-behind-the-ears do-gooder. The only way to deal with the situation was to bide my time until I was released, then put the bastard in the ground.

Just by chance and completely out of the blue, a staff nurse informed me that Ronnie Kray had come to visit. I'd had a run-in with Ron and Reg in the past over one of their henchmen, a man by the name of Willie Malone. He was a trusted member of the twins' firm and if you fucked with one of the firm then you fucked with the Krays. I'd done just that. I'd had a row with Malone and one thing had led to another, resulting in Malone smashing me in the mouth with the butt of his gun. Normally, I would have gone mad, but I had been friends with Malone for some time, so I didn't retaliate. I walked away, but from then on I always carried a gun. I knew when the day finally arrived when I took on Malone, I would bring a whole heap of trouble on myself, but so what? I wanted revenge and vowed one day I'd get it.

My day of reckoning came on the steps of a church in Whitechapel when I spotted Malone talking to some friends. I was aware that Malone always carried a knife, so I looked around in my car for something to use as a weapon. All I could find was an aluminium box spanner. Malone never stood a chance as I beat him to the ground. His friends stepped back, but one hissed, 'You're dead, Shaw,' as I walked away.

I knew I had to be ready for the consequences, and it took just two nights. I was at a mate's basement flat at around 2.30am when we heard footsteps. It was Malone. He'd come to talk, but he had an attitude, one I didn't like, and when he saw me holding a gun he sneered, 'There's no need to point that gun. If you want to shoot me, then shoot me.'

I didn't hesitate. 'OK. I will.'

I pulled the hammer back on the gun and aimed it at Malone's head. My mate panicked. At the time, I thought he feared I'd kill Malone, but it wasn't that at all. He pushed my arm towards the ceiling just as the gun fired.

'No, Roy. It's my settee, it's new. My missus will kill me ...'

Malone and I patched up our differences, but there was unfinished business between me and the Kray twins so I was surprised when Ronnie came to visit me in Broadmoor. This was 1965, long before Ronnie was sentenced to life imprisonment. It was during that visit Ronnie asked me if there was anything he could do for me.

I told him about my wife and that she was having an affair with a plumber. I said I wanted the bastard hurt and hurt bad. He had taken a liberty and I wanted revenge. Ronnie didn't hesitate. 'Consider it done,' he said. 'Don't worry about anything, Roy, I'll take care of it.'

Ron came to see me a few days later. He was true to his word. Quietly, he whispered, 'It's done. The slag's been shot.' From that day on, I have always had the utmost respect for the man. If Ronnie Kray said he would do something, you knew he'd do it. He was a real man, a man of his word.

So that was that. Carolina had gone. I switched off my emotions as easy as switching off a light. Looking back now, I buried my grief and my anger, or should I say I concealed my feelings, but by doing so I found no remedy. When I arrived in Broadmoor I thought I had sunk as low as a man possibly could. I was wrong. I was heading for the bowels of the earth, Broadmoor's dungeons – the punishment block. I was on the edge of the pit of despair just waiting for one little push to send me hurtling, and that little push came from another patient just after breakfast.

The patient was a big lump, built like an ox and twice as ugly. He kept standing in front of me, puffing out his chest with an arrogant look on his face. I couldn't be bothered with him and looked away, but he was having none of it. He took his shirt off, and his body odour made me retch. He flexed his arm muscles and growled: 'My arms are bigger than yours.' His bad breath was foul. I turned the other cheek and walked away.

I went into the toilet and he followed me. I sat in the small cubicle with the door closed but, like most toilets, there was a space under the door to see if anyone was in there. He stood outside the cubicle mumbling and cursing. I sat on the toilet with my head in my hands. I just wanted him to leave me alone.

Suddenly, he opened the toilet door and stood in the doorway. He put his arms up and said again that his arms were bigger than mine. I told him to get out and shut the door. He didn't move so I yelled at him, 'GET OUT AND SHUT THE FUCKING DOOR.'

With no warning he attacked me while I was sitting on the toilet. He punched me in the face, my head jerked back. I looked him in the eyes and stared insanity in the face.

With my trousers still round my ankles I leapt from the toilet and head-butted him. He fell backwards out of the cubicle and banged his head on the wash basin, which gave me time to pull my trousers up. I grabbed him by the throat and smashed his head on the concrete floor. I sat astride him holding him by his windpipe clubbing him in the face again and again. His nose cracked, his teeth broke, his eyes closed. I walked away pulling his front tooth from my knuckles.

Later in the day, I was called in front of the doctor. He asked me about the incident in the toilet. I didn't answer him. He looked at my hands and asked how I had grazed my knuckles. I didn't answer him. He was losing his rag and said, 'I'll ask you for the final time, Roy. How did you hurt your knuckles?' I didn't answer him.

The doctor shrugged his shoulders, 'If that's how you want it,' and rang a concealed buzzer on his desk. Immediately, six screws came into the room and surrounded me. I knew where they would take me – the punishment block. My instincts were to run, but I had nowhere to go. They started grabbing me, so I lashed out and shattered the Governor's cheekbone.

There was an almighty tussle, until one officer managed to slip his arm around my neck and squeezed until I passed out.

I woke up just as I was about to be slung in a dungeon, and I started kicking out. A screw had a syringe prepared in his mouth. I felt a sharp jab in my bum and started to feel drowsy. It gave me enough time to look into their faces and whisper, 'I'm going to do every last one of ya.'

I was in the dungeons – better known as the punishment block – so called because the cells were underground. The official name was the refractory block, and reserved for the nut-nut-nuts.

I lay on a small bed. The shutters were closed, leaving it completely dark except for an observation hole which let in a shaft of light across the floor. Every four hours I was injected with a new drug called Serenade, but it didn't make me sing, it made me hallucinate. It is difficult for me to describe what I felt or to make any sense of it. I was totally debilitated, unable to move my arms and legs, and everything that was happening to me was happening in my head. In my mind's eye, a simple house fly buzzing around the cell became a monster, the fly's movements became exaggerated. I watched it land on the end of the bed and preen itself. I watched the saliva trickle from its mouth, its huge eyes watched me, waiting for the opportunity to pounce. It seemed like I watched it for hours, hardly daring to breathe or blink my eyes. It sounds daft talking about it now, and more daft writing about it, but mind-blowing drugs played mind-blowing games. At the time it was real, terrifyingly real.

Every time I was injected I tried to fight off the effects, I could feel the cold liquid racing through my veins until it reached my brain, making my head spin as fast as a tornado.

After the second injection the fight had left me and the rage had gone. I was given untold injections in my time in solitary, in fact, I lost count. I'm sure they experimented on me, different drugs had different side-effects, some worse than others. But there was one experiment that I will never forget.

My perception of time had deteriorated. I didn't know if it was day or night when my cell door opened and a doctor walked in pushing a trolley, with two male nurses accompanying him. I looked at the trolley and saw a long syringe. It was huge, much larger than usual.

The two male nurses stood either side of me and held my head. I couldn't move my arms, legs or head, I was totally at their mercy, only able to move my eyes. I was so doped up I didn't have control of my mouth, it was as if I'd had ten fillings. The doctor picked up the syringe from the kidney-shaped dish and walked towards me. I tried to spit at him as he leaned over me, but my mouth was dry. The nurses held my head tighter and tighter, it felt like they were crushing my skull.

The doctor smiled and said, 'We are just going to investigate the movement of your brain, Roy.'

He brought the syringe down close to my face. I held my breath as he flicked the needle underneath my cheekbone trying to find a soft point.

'Keep very still, Roy,' he said slowly.

With no more words I felt him push the needle up through my cheek. I felt it go through the gristle and behind my eye. I was rigid with fear.

My whole body tensed as I tried to rise up with the needle to stop him, but the needle continued anyway, pushing behind my eyeball and into my brain. With one final sigh I passed out.

I was kept in the dungeons and allowed no visitors for six months. Even though I was doped up to the eyeballs, I could still remember the faces of the eight screws who put me there. Every time one of those eight men were on duty, I took my chance to hurt them. I had to be assisted from my cell to enable me to use the toilet. It was then I seized the opportunity to seek my revenge. No matter how doped up I was, I had to have a go. I will never forget what they did to me, and just like an elephant I never did.

One morning when a cleaner came into my cell, he said Tom was on duty. Tom was one of the screws who'd taken me over to the dungeon. I remember him vividly kicking me in the back with his size nine boots. He was a nasty, vindictive little bastard, probably the worst screw of all. Even though I was as weak as a kitten, I decided that today was the day Tom was going to cop it.

Late in the afternoon, Tom came into my cell with my tea of sardines on a tin plate. He sneered at me as he handed me the tray. Although I was still groggy, I couldn't resist it. I pushed the plate and the sardines into his face. Then I head-butted his already flat nose and knocked him backwards. That was all I was capable of doing because I was so doped up I could hardly stand. Tom screamed like a schoolgirl. He was big and tough when he was with his mates, but on his own he was like a cry-baby.

Hearing his pitiful cries, the orderlies ran into the cell and overpowered me. They kicked me around a bit and pumped me full of more drugs, but it was worth it.

I stayed in a half-conscious state for months, then a pal of mine on the outside stepped in and saved my life. His name is Joey Pyle. Joey was then, and still is today, a shrewd businessman. If you're lucky enough to make a friend of Joey Pyle then he'll be your friend for life. Joey is an entrepreneur and in the Sixties was responsible, amongst other things, for bringing to this country the World Heavyweight Champion boxer Joe Louis, nicknamed 'The Brown Bomber'. Today's equivalent is Mike Tyson.

A few months into my sentence, Joey Pyle brought The Brown Bomber into Broadmoor to visit me. Everybody made such a fuss, even the Governor. You can imagine today if Mike Tyson was to come to this country and visit an inmate in Broadmoor, there would be an almighty furore.

Everyone enthused about his visit, including Governor Sands. Joey Pyle is a very clever man. He knew by bringing Joe Louis and Terry Downs to visit it would draw attention to me, preventing Broadmoor from turning me into a cabbage or worse still, killing me. Broadmoor and Governor Sands received lots of publicity from Joe Louis' visit, and Governor Sands even became a bit of a star. Joey Pyle was the boxer's promoter and so Governor Sands had many dealings with him. But Joey didn't give a fuck for the Governor or Broadmoor, it was just his way of getting what he wanted. It worked. Governor Sands was confident enough to go out for an evening with Joey to the Astor Club in the West End. He didn't know Joey was a gangster and never had a clue who he was dealing with.

Joey chose his moment carefully before slipping my name into the conversation. The Governor replied, 'If Roy carries on the way he is, he could end up dead within a month.'

He told Joey I was so violent and so uncontrollable they were giving me injections of the strongest drug every four hours. Joey knew he had to get me out of the punishment block and quickly, but there no way the Governor could get Joey in to see me, he was too high profile. It had to be someone I knew, but less well known and someone we trusted. So it was all decided over a table in the Astor Club that Sulky, the owner of the club, would be allowed in to visit me. He would be smuggled into Broadmoor in the dead of the night and allowed to talk to me and to warn me to behave or else they would kill me.

I hadn't seen a friendly face for what seemed an eternity. My cell door opened. In a haze, I looked towards the door, the bright lights hurting my eyes. Standing in the doorway was Sulky. I couldn't believe it. I blinked and blinked again, I thought I was hallucinating.

'You've got five minutes,' I heard someone snap.

Sulky came over to where I was lying and pushed the hair out of my eyes. He was shocked at the state I was in.

'Roy, me old mate, you've got to stop this nonsense ... Joey's asked me to warn you, to tell you could be dead within the month. Think about what you're doing, you'll never win. Please tell the doctors you won't do any more screws.'

I could barely speak but I heard what he said. With one final hug, he left the cell with his head bowed.

All night I thought about what Sulky had said and decided to take his advice. Early in the morning I asked to see the doctor. I told him I wouldn't hurt anyone else, I just wanted to do my bird and get out. He seemed suspicious and said that we would take one step at a time and see how it went.

The next morning my cell was unlocked and in walked one of the screws I'd been attacking. He wished me a good morning, I did the same. The next morning, Scottie came into my cell. He also wished me a good morning. Again, I did the same. I knew they were just testing me. It went on for two weeks and I never touched one of them. After a fortnight, I was trusted out of my cell on to the solitary ward. My medication was decreased, too. I started to feel better, stronger. Six weeks later I heard that Sulky had died. I was saddened that I never got the chance to thank him for coming to see me.

I met other patients who'd been locked in the dungeons, some who'd been far less fortunate than me. One poor soul who was on the Serenade drug had ground his teeth down to the gums.

It was on the solitary wing that I caught up with a friend of mine, a Scot called Jock Hainey. When Jock and I first met in prison, he was a right handful and continually knocked out screws. I heard through the prison grapevine that he'd been sent to Broadmoor. When I saw him, he was a mere shadow of the old bruiser that I used to know. Poor old Jock had been injected straight into his liver. He was a cabbage in every sense of the word and was unable to control any of his bodily functions, even the saliva in his mouth, he was like a baby, completely helpless. I wouldn't have wanted to live that way and I'm sure Jock wouldn't have wanted it either.

I spoke to the doctor and voiced my concerns about Jock. Eventually, his medication was decreased but I think it was too late – the damage to his brain was already done.

Another patient I met in the dungeons was an inmate called Graham Young, the notorious poisoner. From the age of 11, Graham was consumed by a single passion – poison. Anyone he came into contact with – his family, friends or workmates – risked agonising illness and death from his deadly experiments. Graham was first sent to Broadmoor at the tender age of 14 for poisoning his stepmother, who'd died an agonising death. At his trial, he also confessed to poisoning his father, sister and schoolfriend, and although they were very sick, none died. Graham was one of the three youngest males sent to Broadmoor this century.

Being confined did not, however, deter him from his passion because a month after his arrival at Broadmoor, an inmate called John Berridge suffered convulsions and died of cyanide poisoning. I'm sure it was just pure coincidence that he shared the same ward as Graham. Give the man the benefit of the doubt, that's what I always say. Unfortunately for the staff at Broadmoor, they'd also given him the benefit of the doubt, and were taken in by his smooth-talking ways and foolishly gave him the job as tea boy. Unbeknown to the staff, he would pick dandelions and different leaves then mix them up into some sort of poisonous concoction. He was only tumbled when the staff started to fall ill. Fancy giving the job of teaboy to a convicted poisoner. It's like giving a prostitute to Jack the Ripper, or the safe-keys to a bank robber. Who's the crazier? The staff or the poisoner?

I met Graham while we were in solitary. I got on well with him and we became friends when he asked me to look after him because another inmate had threatened him. He was an interesting bloke, although I can't say I understood him.

He was a mine of information and knew a thousand ways of poisoning people and talked about it openly. He had a few visitors, one of whom was his sister, the one he'd tried to poison. She used to bring him homemade cakes. When he came back to the ward he always offered me a slice, but I always declined, and he would laugh. He had a wicked sense of humour, and every day

Another day in the office – with Joe Pyle (*left*) and Alex Steen.

Top: How things might have been ... but unfortunately Donnie 'The Bull' Adams and I had to use gloves.

Bottom: A couple of bruisers, Frankie Fraser and me.

The lovely Sharon – we are still good friends.

Top: 'A word in your ear, Paddy.'

Bottom: The Math Twins, Garry and Steve, 'Mad' Frankie Fraser, Peter and me.

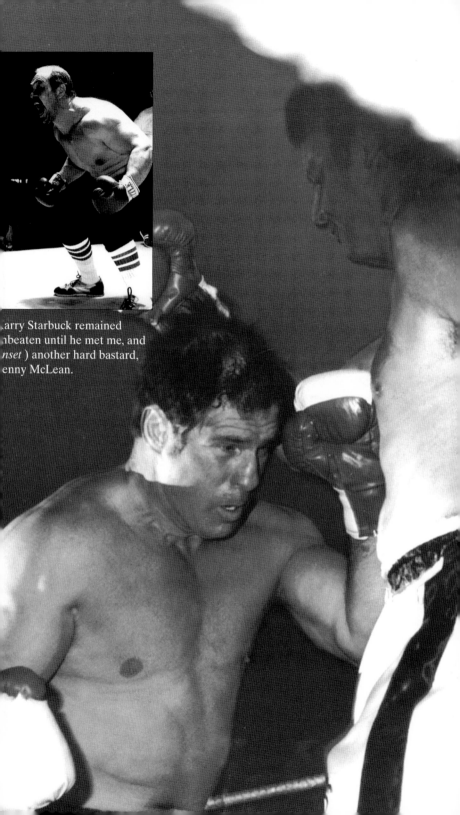

Larry Starbuck remained unbeaten until he met me, and (inset) another hard bastard, Lenny McLean.

Patsy, Rocky and me outside my house in Essex.

Top: Sipping champagne on the Orient Express during the 'world tour' with Patsy.

Bottom: Christmas '98 – a visit to Ronnie Biggs in Brazil.

Me posing.

when the tea urn was brought on to the ward he would chuckle and ask me, 'What's your poison, Roy?'

Shortly after, Graham was moved to another part of the hospital and I never saw him again, but I always kept an eye on the papers when his name was mentioned.

I'd snigger at the fact that so many people were taken in by him and gave him the benefit of the doubt. In 1970, psychiatrists said that Graham was reformed and he was released back into the community in 1971. He started work at a factory in Herefordshire. Within a month, six colleagues fell ill with mysterious symptoms, and within six months two workmates were dead. Graham Young was charged with their murders and was sentenced to life imprisonment. Instead of returning him to Broadmoor, he was transferred to Parkhurst, the maximum security jail on the Isle of Wight, and there he stayed until August 1990 when he died of a heart-attack at the age of 42. I sometimes wondered if he'd taken one of his poisonous concoctions himself. He was to be known as the worst poisoner this century, and was immortalised in wax in Madame Tussaud's Chamber of Horrors.

This achievement was one of Graham's greatest ambitions and he often spoke about it while we were together in the dungeons. There is a fine line between intelligence and insanity. Graham Young had a bit of both, but I'd say his mind was definitely poisoned.

After nine months in the dungeons I was finally taken back to Block 7, and back to my old cell. I can't say I was glad to be 'home', but after spending so long in the dungeon my cell looked pretty damn good. Now that was frightening. If I thought a cell in Broadmoor looked good there was definitely something wrong. Before I knew it, I'd done five years in Broadmoor; I had to get a grip and sort my life out. More importantly, I had to get out.

My yearly tribunal was due to discuss my progress and my future. I asked to see Dr McGrath, the chief doctor, who looked after all the parole patients. I talked with him about the possibility of being transferred to a county hospital, which is a medium-risk unit, a stepping-stone to freedom. He catagorically refused. He explained that it was out of the question because no hospital was prepared to take me because of my record. He wouldn't elaborate; he just said my record was too bad. My only option was to return to prison, and then out.

I couldn't get that report out of my mind. What had I done that was so bad? For weeks I kept thinking about it, and it really bugged me. I had to get my hands on my report – if I knew what was in it, then I could remedy it.

Once out of solitary and back on the ward, everything seemed less stressful. The screws even seemed friendlier. One in particular was OK, his name was Alf, and he'd been working in Broadmoor for donkey's years and knew the score. In actual fact, screws could be bought for two bob. If you have enough money, anything can be bought, because money talks.

I asked Alf if he could get my records for me to read. He scratched his chin and shook his head, 'Well, I'll see what I can do ...' It was a case of nudge-nudge, wink-wink, before he added, 'It'll cost ya ...'

We agreed a price there and then. Two days later, I had my records in my hand. As I thumbed through the pages of the folder, I was amazed at its contents. It made shocking reading. It was like reading about a stranger, a maniac, a madman. Anyone but me.

My whole life history was in a folder five inches thick. Every violent incident that I had been involved in was written up and logged in chronological order. I felt sick as I read the pages one by one, each report was handwritten in such detail and it was exaggerated out of all proportion. At the end of each report was a summary written in red – a forewarning, I presume.

After each incident, the report concluded that the officer involved feared for his life, and even the doctor in Grendon Underwood whom I'd thought was OK and had my best interests at heart, had no faith in me. I was shocked at what he wrote in big red letters: 'SHAW IS THE MOST POWERFUL AND DANGEROUS MAN I HAVE ATTEMPTED TO TREAT.'

The doctor was in charge of all the psychiatric prisons in the country. His recommendations were final. So what chance did I have of ever getting out with a record like mine? I handed the report back to Alf with a feeling of utter despair and desolation. Alf was a shrewd old bastard and sensed my feeling of hopelessness.

'Don't worry, Roy,' he said. 'All the time you have breath in your body there's always a chance of freedom.'

I smiled. Those were the exact words I'd said to Billy Doyle when he asked me to kill him. I'd tried to give Billy Doyle false hope and Alf was trying to do the same for me, and look what happened to Billy Doyle. Well, there was no way I was leaving Broadmoor in a body bag, I had to take drastic action before it was too late.

I decided on a rooftop protest to make the powers-that-be sit up and take notice, which was easier said than done. The only time I was allowed off the ward was for a visit, so I arranged for a trusted friend to come to see me, and to bring a couple of items that I might need. I knew a gun and a knife were out of the question, no one could smuggle that through the security, but a length of string was all I'd require. I told my visitor my intentions and asked him to inform the newspapers of my grievances. Going on to the roof seemed to me to be the only way of making the authorities listen.

Broadmoor has strict guidelines on patients and visitors, never allowing the visitors to leave the hall at the same time as the patients. Either the patient is escorted out first or the visitor, but they are never in the grounds at the same time, for fear of confusion and escape.

After the visit, I said goodbye to my friend, we shook hands and I waited to be taken back. We purposely finished our visit 20 minutes early; that way, I would be escorted back to the ward alone.

Two screws accompanied me down the long corridor to the heavily barred gate out into the small courtyard. I waited while they unlocked the gate, chatting together as if I wasn't there, as if I was invisible. This added to my determination and conviction that what I was about to do was my only option.

Once across the courtyard and through the second gate I

seized my chance. I gave the guards the slip and ran across the grass. I jumped over the rosebushes, over the privet hedge, and over a garden bench, keeping my eyes fixed firmly on a drain pipe. I knew exactly where I was heading.

The guards were in hot pursusit. I shinned up the drainpipe before they had even made it across the grass. They were shouting at me to stop, but it was too late – I was already on the roof. The officers were furious; by giving them the slip, I'd put their jobs in jeopardy. I laughed and shouted at them, 'TAKE NOTICE OF ME NOW, YOU SLAGS.'

They were absolutely livid, spitting feathers and swearing at me. One of the officers shouted at the top of his voice, 'GET THE FUCK OFF THAT ROOF, SHAW.'

I balanced on the ridge tiles like a trapeze artist waving my arms in the air laughing and jeering, then threw a slate at the officers. It just missed one of them. I let out a raucous laugh. Standing on the ridge tiles, it felt good to be in control again. It was like being on top of the world, I could see for miles. I took a deep breath and held it. I felt alive and free and fucking marvellous.

I continued to rip slates from the roof and hurled them at the officers telling them all to fuck off. In no time at all, the siren was sounded indicating a prisoner on the loose. The siren at Broadmoor is very distinct and very loud and, apart from when it is tested every Monday morning, the only other time it is heard is when an inmate has escaped, warning the surrounding village of the imminent danger.

I stayed on the roof for hours, taunting and jeering the gathered crowd, and as soon as it started to get dark a floodlight was turned on. It was so strong the light hurt my eyes but I didn't care, I stood in the beam and in true Hollywood style burst into song: 'Up on the roof ... Up on the roof ... When this old world starts getting you down ...'

I looked down into the courtyard at my audience and gave a gracious bow as if in a Gala performance in front of royalty. As Queen Victoria would have said, 'They were not amused.'

Everyone was running around, not really knowing what to do. Police, screws and snarling dogs had surrounded the building. A psychiatrist with a megaphone shouted muffled messages at me, 'COME DOWN, ROY, AND WE WILL FORGET ALL ABOUT IT. YOU WILL NOT, REPEAT NOT, BE IN ANY TROUBLE.'

I just threw a couple of slates at him and told him to shove it up his arse. My euphoria was short-lived as there is only just so much singing and dancing a man can do, especially on a rooftop. By 1.00am I was exhausted. It was freezing. I knew the authorities were playing a waiting game.

I tried to keep awake but I was getting very tired. I decided to tie myself to a chimney pot so I could have a nap; that way I wouldn't fall off. I knew that length of string would come in handy. Obviously, I didn't get any sleep as it was too cold. I was just glad it didn't rain. By the second day, I was cold and hungry. I'd made my point and it was time to come down.

I put my hands up indicating I'd had enough. My feet never touched the ground. I was taken directly to the dungeons and back to square one. Dr McGrath came to see me and asked me why I'd felt the need to do a rooftop protest. I told him that I wanted to go back to prison to finish off my sentence, that I'd had enough of Broadmoor. I'd been there for five years. I'd heard that Billy Curbishly and the others were home. If I stayed in Broadmoor, I feared I'd be there indefinitely.

Dr McGrath said that he would talk to the Governor and see what he could do, but he was promising nothing. To this day, I'm not sure if it was my rooftop protest or the fact that Joey Pyle had intervened, or maybe Broadmoor was just glad to see the back of me. Who knows and who cares what the reason was? All I know is that within the week I was leaving Broadmoor, and on a ferry bound for Parkhurst – and if I was looking for trouble, I was heading for the right place.

CHAPTER 9

BROWN BREAD

'I had to go to the Reception Wing where there was a full-length mirror. As I walked past, I caught a glimpse of myself. I stopped dead in my tracks and took a double-take. I was as wide as I was tall and resembled an Oxo cube ...'

IT WAS AUGUST 1970. Finally, I was on my way to Parkhurst Prison on the Isle of Wight. I thought I'd left my troubles behind me in Broadmoor. Wrong, wrong, wrong. I felt slightly seasick as I sat between two screws on a wind-swept deck on the Portsmouth to Ryde ferry. The English Channel was choppy, and the ferry rolled with each wave. I should have read it as a bad omen that going back to prison wasn't going to be all plain sailing, and little did I know that I was sailing full steam ahead into stormy waters.

I had been in prison since 1963. So many unspeakable things had happened to me in that time. The fights, the rages, the solitary, being imprisoned in the dungeons for nine months and, worst of all, being experimented on with mind-blowing drugs. It's a wonder I wasn't stark raving mad.

I was handcuffed between two officers, feeling quiet and subdued. I hadn't been on a bus or in a car, let alone a ferry, for so long. In fact, I hadn't walked any faster than a trot for seven years. Everything on the outside world changes at an alarming rate; everything seemed faster, or was I just slower? It's something only another prisoner would recognise, the feeling of loneliness, not because I was alone but lonely in my mind. I felt detached from the real world as if I didn't belong. I thought everyone knew where I had been and where I was going, as if there was a neon sign over my head saying: 'CAUTION – BEWARE'.

I looked at the other passengers going about their business. There was an old couple sitting on a bench huddled together to keep warm. They had probably been married for years and were perhaps going to visit their grandchildren with a pocketful of sweets. I watched a boisterous youngster break free from his mother's grip, shrieking with delight when she chased him across the deck. But above all, what grabbed my attention the most were the girls, or more specifically their skirts – mini skirts. They were short, boy, were they short! Almost indecent. I couldn't take my eyes off them. One pretty little thing in particular kept walking past, smiling sweetly.

A guard nudged me. 'Look at her legs, Roy, right up to her armpits.' He shook his head and sighed. 'See what you've been missing.'

I was in a trance, I couldn't take my eyes off the girls, I was mesmerised like a stoat by a snake, and when the sweetheart skipped up the steps to the top deck I thought I'd have a heart-attack. The guard was right, dead right. I had missed so much while inside, up until that point I never realised that things had changed so much. It's not a conscious thought but when you are imprisoned you assume that life on the outside stands still. Wrong. Time waits for no man. I was put away in 1963 just as the country was starting to wake up, and by 1970 the country was wide awake and raring to go, but I had been a hibernating bear – a bear with a sore head.

I arrived at Parkhurst just after dark. I was taken directly to Block B and banged up for the night. The next morning I stepped out on to the landing expecting ... expecting ... hmmm ... I don't know what I was expecting. Changes? Strangers? A row?

While things changed on the outside, on the inside everything stayed the same.

'All right, Roy?' someone shouted.

I looked around to see where the voice was coming from. A familiar face beamed at me across the landing. It was an old mate from the Scrubs.

'All right, mate. How ya doin'?' I answered. 'Thought you'd be out by now. You only had two years to start.'

'Nah, nah. I'm doing ten now,' he bragged.

Someone else called, 'Hello, Roy.' I recognised another motley inmate. 'I'm doing 18,' he said, smiling.

And so it went on. It was the same old faces, just different places. It was as if I had never been away. I collected my breakfast and went back to my cell. It made me think very seriously about what sort of a life you have when it is measured by the length of time served in prison. Prison is a mug's game, it's a complete waste of time and a complete waste of your life.

I only had three years left on my sentence and with parole perhaps only 12 to 18 months. I decided to knuckle down and get back into training. I started lifting heavy weights and became fit and strong. I even entered a weightlifting competition between some of the prisons. The finalists were whittled down to three prisoners, all from Parkhurst. Me, a geezer called Fruin and Reggie Kray. Reggie was in a different block to me because he was a lifer. He was strong for his weight, and extremely fit. I was 16 stone and at the peak of my physical fitness. Without realising it, I'd bulked out and had become massive. I hadn't seen my reflection because in prison the only mirror available is a small shaving mirror, so you never see the rest of your body.

For some reason, I can't remember what, I had to go to the Reception Wing where there was a full-length mirror. As I walked past, I caught a glimpse of myself. I stopped dead in my tracks and took a double-take. I stood in front of the mirror and gawped. I was shocked and surprised at the size I had become. I was as wide as I was tall and resembled an Oxo cube. I puffed my chest out and shook my tail feathers singing, 'I feel good ... doodle loodle loodle loo.'

I didn't have long to go before my parole. I was looking and feeling good and for the first time in a long while I could see the light at the end of the tunnel. I really thought I was over the worst, that all my troubles were packed up in my old kit bag and they were done and dusted. Again, I was wrong. When I opened my kit bag to get my football boots, trouble spewed out with them, big trouble, in the guise of another inmate, Mr Brown. I don't remember what his first name was, nor do I care. The important thing, though, is that he was soon to be 'brown bread'.

I pulled on my football boots that fateful afternoon, completely unaware that by the end of the football game a man would be dead. I ran on to the pitch with an old mate called Bertie Coster, who was doing seven years for robbery. Bert was a good-looking man with olive skin and jet-black hair.

From the moment the game started, it became a grudge match between Bertie Coster and Mr Brown. And the latter was a fucking nuisance on the football pitch.

If he fouled Bert once, he fouled him a dozen times. Bert got the needle and a few words, as well as a few blows, were exchanged. After the football match, on the way back to the wing Bert told me he was going to bash Mr Brown. I told Bert to leave it, to bide his time and wait.

As we went through the tunnel that went from one wing to another, Mr Brown followed us, still obviously angry and wanting to have a go. We could hear him shouting behind us: 'Fucking London gangsters, I've shit 'em.'

At the end of the tunnel we went up the stone steps to reach the floor of the wing. Mr Brown followed behind us all the way through the tunnel cursing and threatening all sorts. By the time we reached the top of the stone steps, Mr Brown felt brave. There was a bit of a tussle, fists were flying in every direction. I can't remember exactly who hit who, but I think Mr Brown must have tripped. Yeah, that's it. He tripped. He fell backwards down the stone steps until he reached the bottom. I told Bert to go, just to get away while he could. I ran down the steps to help Mr Brown.

I picked him up by his jacket, stood him up and propped him against the wall. As I did, he gave out a groan so I let go of his jacket and he fell to his knees. I went back to my cell and waited to have the door unlocked for tea.

For two days, everybody was banged up and not even allowed out for exercise. We all knew the reason why, because of the scuffle on the landing, but we didn't know the severity. As usual on a Sunday night for supper, prisoners were given gorgonzola cheese, a cob of bread and a big mug of tea. I sat on my bunk eating my cheese roll and reading a newspaper.

Suddenly, the door opened. Two officers came in. They asked me what had happened on Friday afternoon after coming in from the football game. They asked if I had seen anything. I said no. They asked if I had seen any trouble. Again I replied no. I said I'd heard that someone had been hurt on the landing and enquired if that person was OK, then nonchalantly took another bite from my cheese roll. Just as they closed my door, a guard muttered, 'He's dead.' The mouthful of food stuck in my throat and I could hardly swallow.

'Brown bread. He's brown bread,' I spluttered.

Later, two police officers returned and charged me with murder. I was put in the chokey with Bert, who was also charged with the murder of Mr Brown. I was transferred to Gartree Prison in Leicester until the trial, then I returned to Parkhurst to face a life sentence for murder. Again, my old friend Joey Pyle stepped in and saved the day. He got me the best solicitor money could buy.

I stood in the dock, my mind full of what might have been. What if this? What if that? Life in prison or, worse still, Broadmoor – indefinitely. If convicted I was in a no-win situation; either way I wouldn't see the light of day for many years. I had to take drastic action, and get out of this mess. Most of the witnesses had been scared off one way or another, through a friend of a friend, and the frighteners had been put on them. Only two eye-witnesses remained.

One of them was brought in to give evidence against us. He

stood in the dock and I glared at him. The prosecution asked him a question. He shuffled from foot to foot, toyed with his hair and pursed his lips before saying, 'Well, it's like this ... Me and my friend were coming back from watching the football.'

I was incensed by his camp voice and effeminate gestures. I stood up and yelled at him to tell the truth.

'Tell 'em what you saw, you fucking poof.'

The magistrates warned me that if there were any more disturbances I would be removed from the court. The witness stood in the dock, shaking all over, and eventually spluttered: 'Er ... er ... all I saw was Shaw helping Brown up from the bottom of the stairs.'

The witness was discharged and never looked back as he minced out of the court, passing the next witness coming in. Everything hinged on what this witness said, or rather what I wanted him to say. He stood in the witness box and started to speak. I never took my eyes off him. If looks could kill he'd also be stone dead. He tried to avoid my menacing gaze, and he might not have looked me straight in the eye but he could feel the bad vibes which hung in the air like a black fog. I waited until he reached the right moment in his evidence then I leapt to my feet and hollered at him to tell the truth.

In that split second, I convinced him to change his story. In a flash, he answered, 'I never saw nuffink, honest, I never saw nuffink.'

The screws jumped on me and grappled me to the floor, trying to silence me but it made no difference. I got the result I wanted. My brief stepped in and seized the opportunity by saying I had no case to answer, all I was guilty of was helping Mr Brown who was so obviously in distress, like any good citizen would. Joey said the solicitor was good, and he was right. I even thought at one point I was going to be recommended for a bravery award.

I was acquitted, thank God. It all turned around, and it could have been so different. For once, Lady Luck was looking down on me. Bert, on the other hand, went on trial for murder. The charge was eventually reduced to manslaughter and Bert received an extra nine months on his sentence.

So that was the end of that. I was shipped out of Parkhurst and back to Gartree in Leicester to finish off the remainder of my sentence. It was while in Gartree that I met Harry Roberts, the notorious cop killer. When you meet Harry, what you see is what you get. He is an intelligent man, a member of Mensa, very articulate and says what he's got to say – whether you like it or not.

In 1966, Harry Roberts was Britain's most wanted man. On Friday, 12 August, in a quiet street near London's Shepherd's Bush, he and two accomplices gunned down three policemen. Until then, the murder of a British policeman was virtually unheard of, let alone three. At his trial, Harry was given three life sentences with a recommendation that he served 30 years before being eligible for parole. As this book goes to print in early 1999, Harry has served nearly 33 years inside with still no date for release.

By the time I caught up with Harry in Gartree, he was already well into his sentence. Harry has tried to escape on many occasions. In actual fact, he has attempted to escape – and failed – 22 times. One such attempt was to spark a riot which was to start me on a journey visiting almost every prison in the country. I was moved every couple of months because I was known as a trouble-maker and thought that I'd be deterred by moving me. Wrong. In all, I went to 21 different prisons for 21 different reasons.

But what started the ball rolling was Harry Roberts and a couple of IRA men as they made a dash for the outer fence of Gartree Prison. For weeks, there had been talk on the wing of an escape attempt. So when the alarms were sounded, bells rang and whistles blew, I knew what was going down. I stood on my chair and looked out of my cell window and saw the desperadoes run across the yard and begin to scramble up the fence. Almost every screw in the nick was in hot pursuit. All the prisoners were yelling out of their windows, geeing them along and urging them to escape. From my cell, I could see everything. I watched a screw chase one in particular, his name was Ernie Bell. I don't know what Ernie was in for and it wasn't the done thing to ask, but whatever it was he didn't deserve what he was about to receive. Ernie was halfway up the fence, when the screw grabbed him by the legs and tugged. Ernie fell into the courtyard, the screw pulled out his truncheon and smashed Ernie's head in. He didn't just use reasonable force, he was brutal.

Other prisoners who had been watching the incident were incensed by the toe-curling ferocity that the screw exerted on Ernie. There was an almighty outcry from the inmates as the screw continued hammering at Ernie's lifeless body. Animal instincts took over and we reacted the only way we knew how.

Without any prompting or discussion, each and every man took revenge by demolishing his cell. We were all swept away on a tide of emotion, the noise was deafening. Alarm bells were ringing, men were shouting and ripping out sinks, smashing up furniture. All the pent-up frustration that had been building up in Gartree Prison came to a head. The screws scrambled out of the wing as quickly as they could, locking us inside.

We responded by barricading the doors and rampaging through the wing, demolishing tables and chairs and anything else that got in our way, and leaving a trail of destruction behind us. The pressure was explosive, nothing was going to stop us. We destroyed everything we could lay our hands on.

Desperate men use desperate measures, and once we had smashed all there was to smash we started on the cell doors. It soon became apparent that if you put a book between a cell door and the post and slammed it hard, the door breaks the hinges off leaving a big heavy door that can be used as a battering ram. Half a dozen men held on to the heavy door and methodically slammed it again and again into a brick wall until it eventually went right through which enabled us to make our way to the floor where the strong box was holding 'Mad' Frankie Fraser. Frankie had been kept in the strongbox for weeks, and was an old hand in the art of solitary confinement. Nothing and nobody phased him, he was a man who operated through a mixture of fear and charm.

He didn't get the name 'Mad Frank' for nothing. He earned it, and if you cross him, you do so at your peril. If you attack Frankie, you had better hope that you kill him, otherwise, make no mistake, he will come after you and cut your throat.

I called to Frankie and told him that I would have him out in a jiff. I kept smashing the glass roof until it broke. Frankie was sitting on the concrete floor looking up. He was a wiry old fox totally unperturbed by all the commotion going on around him. I really thought that Frankie would want to get out. Wrong. I held my arm out eager to haul Frankie to freedom. He shook his head majestically.

'No, Roy,' he said quietly. 'Don't be so silly, you'll only get yourself into trouble.'

I laughed. 'Get into trouble, Frank? I've just demolished half the fucking prison.' Frankie was adamant that he was going nowhere. I tried to persuade him but he was having none of it, so I said, 'If you don't want to come out, what the fuck do you want?'

Frankie paused and thought for a moment. 'I want a nice cup of coffee, Roy. That's what I want, a nice cup of coffee.'

I stood on top of the strongbox, sweating, exhausted, and covered in brick dust, and Frankie wanted a cup of coffee. Well, a cup of coffee he would have. I left Frankie in the strongbox drinking his brew, and walked away shaking my head in disbelief. Coffee in the strongbox, it's never been known before, or since, I suspect.

We continued to run amok for two days. We smashed all there was to smash, wrecked all there was to wreck and, to be honest, we burnt ourselves out. The authorities knew the riot couldn't continue indefinitely, so they sat back and waited for it to fizzle out. There were no come-backs, no retribution, at least, not that I know of, because the next day I was moved out to Hull Prison.

Going to Hull didn't bother me a jot. They could send me anywhere they wanted and it bothered me not. Fuck me, I've turned into Shakespeare.

There were many familiar faces in Hull. I was just biding my time until my release but even something as simple as watching the Olympics on the television turned into a fiasco. Me and a couple of mates only wanted to watch the boxing, that wasn't too much to ask. We weren't doing any harm to anyone. It was nearly time to be banged up for the night when a screw walked, or rather marched, into the TV room with an attitude, a bad attitude, and told us to go to bed. We weren't children, we were fully grown, roughie, toughie prisoners. I asked politely if we could finish watching the boxing. Just because we were prisoners didn't mean we weren't patriotic, we supported our country, after all we were being held at Her Majesty's pleasure. It didn't mean to say we didn't love our Queen and Country, a more patriotric motley old bunch of lags could not be found anywhere. I foolishly thought the screw might exercise a bit of discretion, work on his own initiative for once, be a man. Banish that thought. There's no such thing as a screw with initiative. There was no reasoning with the man, he didn't even want to think about it for a moment, he just said no.

So I did no more than tell him to fuck off and take his attitude with him. We weren't going anywhere, we were watching the boxing and that was that.

Within minutes, the PO walked in. He didn't look at us, acknowledge us or say a word, he just bent down to pull the TV plug out of the wall. I leant back in my chair, put my arms behind my head and growled, 'Touch that plug and I'll break your fucking neck.'

He froze like a statue.

'Think very carefully,' I said slowly.

I could almost hear his brain ticking over. Shall I? Shan't I? For a moment he thought long and hard. He made the right decision. The boys cheered as the PO walked out of the TV room with his tail between his legs.

Day and night for two days, we watched the Olympics. On the third day, tired and exhausted, with square eyes from watching too much TV, I was moved to Durham prison. I hadn't even unpacked my bits and pieces, I'd literally walked in and sat on my bunk when the Governor and a screw walked in. The screw snarled, 'On your feet for the Governor.'

I sighed. Another nick, another row. I didn't even look up, I just growled, 'Fuck the Governor.'

As it happened, it was the same Governor Frankie Fraser had done a few years back. Now the Governor had the hump and shouted at me, 'Get on your feet, Shaw.'

I was weary and tired of the whole charade. I hauled my weary carcass off the bunk and stood toe-to-toe with the Governor and hissed, 'Fuck off and leave me alone or I'll do more to you than Frankie Fraser ever did.'

You could have heard a pin drop as he turned and closed the door.

I spent my month or so in Durham prison banged up most of the time. That was just fine and fucking dandy with me, I needed a break.

Then I was moved to Leicester Prison for a while, then another jail, then another, then another. Every nick I was moved to I asked the Governor the same question, 'Do you want any trouble in your prison?' Each and every Governor's reply was the same – no. I told them all I wanted was my weights in my cell for an hour every day. I politely explained that I had to rid myself of aggression otherwise I'd take it out on the screws. They only had to look at my record to know I meant what I said.

I had moved to so many different jails that I lost track, all I wanted to do was serve my time and get out. The last Governor I delivered my well-rehearsed speech to actually listened to me. He couldn't understand why I had been moved from prison to prison and assured me he would look into it. Three weeks later, off I went again, this time to Long Lartin maximum security jail in Evesham, Worcester. It was a brand-spanking-new nick and had only just opened. It was one of those new-wave-fandango 'help the prisoner' nicks full of painting and sculpting classes. I walked into the Reception Wing and was greeted by a smiling prison officer.

'Hello, Roy,' he said.

Now, I thought he was a smiling viper and instantly said, 'Don't call me Roy, my name's Shaw.'

'Not in this prison, Roy.'

I was totally flummoxed. I wasn't used to being treated with kid gloves and I didn't like it, not one bit. I had been used to being at loggerheads with the screws and the authorities and was suspicious and paranoid; almost overnight they had become human. For so long I had had to fight to survive, and I couldn't get used to the softly, softly approach. They tried to make me join in one of the many art classes, then they tried to make me go into one of the workshops, but I wouldn't. I found the cosy approach more difficult to deal with than the usual aggression. It's difficult to whack someone when they are smiling at you. I just couldn't get used to the screws talking to me and calling me by my first name. They even urged me to call them by their first names, but I couldn't. For so many years I considered anyone who was friendly with a screw to be a grass, and that conviction was so deep-rooted inside me that try as I might, I just couldn't lose that notion. Even the Governor was a crank and walked around the nick like an old farmer wearing a cheese-cutter hat and a pair of garish check trousers – smiling, it was as if he was stoned on happy baccy.

Like a square peg in a round hole, I just didn't fit in to Long Lartin's new régime. I knew it, the screws knew it and the wacky Governor certainly knew it. Right out of the blue, the Governor called me into his office and pushed out a chair and asked me to sit down. I told him I preferred to stand. For the first time, he raised his voice, gone was the nice approach, 'Look,' he said. 'You're going to fuck it all up for me.'

He meant his job. I was going to fuck his job up because I wouldn't conform. I just started to protest when he stopped me in my tracks and shouted: 'Look, I'm not supposed to tell you this, but the Home Office has given you parole. In six weeks' time you are going home.'

Home. I couldn't believe it. I was going home. I don't think it sank in straightaway, I'd been inside for ten years. Maybe it was a trick.

'Where am I going to work until I go home?' I asked suspiciously.

'Work? Work where you fucking well like,' he snapped. 'But just keep out of trouble, Shaw.'

At last, I was going home.

The night before my release, I was excited, nervous, apprehensive, but deliriously fucking happy. It was difficult to sleep, so I got up at 4.00am, washed, shaved and was ready to go. The screws gave me a no-return, one-way ticket ... to Dagenham.

CHAPTER 10

PEOPLE TO SEE, PLACES TO GO

'It seemed as if there had been a population explosion, there were so many people of every creed and colour from all walks of life. I was only used to walking the length of the prison landing. I stood in the middle of the busy pavement totally perplexed ...'

THE STEAM TRAIN EMERGED FROM THE TUNNEL in a cloud of smoke, giving a final sigh as it halted at the platform. It was my train back to London – my train home. As I stepped on to the train I knew I was on the right track at last.

'All aboard,' a guard called as the train lurched out of the station and rhythmically chugged faster and faster as it gathered steam. I was thrown from side to side as I made my way up the narrow corridor looking for an empty compartment. For a moment, I paused at the door expecting someone to unlock it. I stumbled backwards as I threw my brown paper parcel containing all my worldly goods on to the parcel shelf then settled back for the long journey to London.

My mind was racing as fast as the train. It was difficult not to judge the future by my past, but I'd dreamt of freedom for ten long years and now I had it, I had to re-define my dream as I intended never to lose my freedom again. I felt different, I was re-entering the game – the game of life, and I didn't want to be the only one left without a chair when the music stopped this time. I must have been getting philosophical in my old age. What am I saying? I was only 37 years old and I had a lot of living and loving to do yet.

I settled back in the seat, wiped the condensation from the window and peered out at the wide open space. I never realised I would appreciate the beauty of freedom and the countryside so much. The autumn leaves were spectacular in their beauty, the vivid colours of burnt umber, russet and gold were unforgettable, a sight so beautiful it made my heart sing. For the first time in my life my eyes were opened to the things that we all take for granted, it was such a marvellous, wonderful feeling and I smiled from ear to ear.

I savoured the moment for most of the journey but as the train headed out of the sticks and into the smoke of London, I came back to earth with a bump. First and foremost I had to get some money and somewhere to live, but the most immediate thought was for my children. I hadn't seen them for so long, and I wondered if they even remembered me. Then there was the little matter of my wife's boyfriend whom I had to take care of. I had people to see and places to go and in order to do these things I had to get some wheels. My first port of call was to a friend of mine in Aldgate who had a garage. He'd written to me and told me that as soon as I got out of prison he would give me a car.

We arrived at Paddington Station and I intended to catch the tube to Aldgate East, but from the moment I stepped off the train, the throng of so many people bustling around, pushing and shoving, made my head spin.

I had to get out of the station quickly, but the main road was worse. Black cabs with irate drivers hooted red buses, which were blocking the cars, which were blocking the motor bikes, which were blocking the pedestrians. It was complete mayhem.

It seemed as if there had been a population explosion, there were so many people of every creed and colour from all walks of life. I was only used to walking the length of the prison landing. I stood in the middle of the busy pavement totally perplexed.

There was no way I could continue my journey by tube, bus or anything else for that matter. I had to get to a phone box to ring my mate to pick me up. I closed the door of the phone box feeling a little safer inside and to my horror discovered that even the phone had changed. I fumbled in my pocket for a coin. Pounds, shillings and pence had given way to decimalisation and I just couldn't get used to the new money.

On my fifth attempt I got through to my mate, Ginger. I told him to pick me up and he would find me in the call box outside the station. I'd written to family and friends to let them know of my release date. Many had offered to pick me up but I declined, because I've never needed anyone to hold my hand, then or since. But I hadn't realised how fast things move on the outside. Since I'd been away, the world had got itself in an awful hurry.

Ginger pulled up outside the call box and tooted his car horn. It was good to see a familiar face. Ginger and his partner Harry had been friends of mine for years. They owned a garage in the Seventies and still do today. They are typical fast-talking, wheeler-dealing, ducking and diving car salesmen.

Ginger drove me to my mum's house and she greeted me with open arms. It was so good to see her again! I picked her up and twirled her round, both of us laughing. But there was something I had to know.

'Where is she?' I whispered. Mum knew straightaway who I meant. Her face changed.

'Don't start any trouble, Roy, she ain't worth it.'

I listened to Mum's protests and pacified her. I respected what she said but I had my pride; my wife had taken a liberty – or should I say, her lover had taken a liberty. It was obvious Mum knew where she lived, because there was no way she wouldn't be in contact with her grandchildren. It took a while before Mum reluctantly gave me Carolina's address. She was living in a block of flats in Rainham, Essex.

I wasted no time and drove across town to see my children. If I thought walking along the pavement was difficult, driving was nigh on impossible, but I was a man on a mission.

I parked the car in the street opposite the flats and walked across the patch of grass. Nearby, a group of children were playing. They were running around squealing, chasing each other and kicking a ball. Suddenly, a little girl dropped the ball and ran towards me with outstretched arms.

'Daddy, Daddy,' she cried.

It was my dear, sweet Chatina. I felt a lump in my throat as tears streamed down my face, for so many years I thought I'd lost her. I don't know how she recognised me. I bent down to pick her up, she threw her arms around me and smothered me in kisses. I felt her warm embrace and as she tugged at my jacket so she tugged at my heart. She didn't know or care where I'd been, she was just so happy I was there.

Then an inquisitive young boy cautiously approached to see what all the fuss was about. It was my son, Gary. I looked at the youngster. He returned my gaze with suspicion. He was so obviously my son, a chip off the old block.

'It's Daddy, Gary. It's Daddy,' Chatina squealed.

His face lit up as he ran to me and clutched me around the waist. I ruffled his hair as my father did to me the last time I saw him. There is nothing in this world like the loving embrace of your own flesh and blood. As I held my children I felt, at last, I belonged to someone and someone belonged to me.

I told the children to go off and play while I spoke to their mum, then I made my way up to the second floor flat. The front door was ajar and I could hear voices. I stood in the cluttered hall, and saw that the first doorway led directly into the kitchen. Quietly I slipped in and listened. Inside the kitchen was a serving hatch which enabled me to see through to the living room. A man was declaring his love.

'But, Carolina, I love you, I want to stay with you.'

I thought I had buried my feelings for Carolina, whom I'd divorced a long while ago, but what the eye doesn't see the heart doesn't grieve over. However, hearing someone else say those words to my ex-wife stung my ears and brought all those feelings flooding back to the surface. I wasn't in a position to take care of lover number one – the plumber – Ronnie Kray had done the honours, but this one was mine, all mine. I was shaking with anger, literally shaking. I walked into the lounge and stood in the doorway. Carolina and a man were sitting on the sofa holding hands. She looked up, and the blood drained from her face.

There was a deathly silence. Quickly she pulled her hand away and stood up. I could see the panic and fear in her eyes as she gasped, 'Roy ... when did you ...? How did you ...? What are you doing here?'

I was so angry I couldn't speak, I just glared at her lover. All I could hear in my mind was him telling Carolina that he loved her. There was no need for introductions, it was obvious who I was, and no mistaking who he was. He was her lover, plain and simple.

He stood up and walked towards me. I put my arm across the doorway blocking his exit. Carolina knew what was coming, but he didn't. He stooped down to get under my arm, and I grabbed him by the seat of his trousers and the collar of his jacket as Carolina screamed. I ran with him up the hallway, out of the front door and threw him straight over the balcony. Carolina screamed hysterically.

I looked over the balcony. He was lying on the concrete below, face down. One leg was folded under his body. Instantly, a stream of claret flowed into the gutter. There was no better place for him, although he didn't die – unfortunately.

That was one problem solved; the second was money, or the lack of it. Word on the street soon got round that I was out of prison and hungry, and I don't mean for food. I had been away for a long while and in that time things had changed. Different faces had moved in on my manor. Well, I was out now and I was going to pick up where I left off and nobody – I mean nobody – was going to stop me.

I was approached by a club owner in Dagenham who was having aggro in his club and couldn't handle it. Some tough guys called the Maxwell Brothers were causing him all sorts of trouble. The owner was scared stiff and was way out of his depth. He wanted to bar them but was too frightened and asked me to clean it up.

'It's the Maxwells. I want them gone. Sort my club out, Roy, and name your price.'

I thought about it. I could sort his club out, no problem. It wasn't really my line of work but I could do this as well as almost anything else. I smiled and said, 'Maybe.' I thought about it for at least ten seconds. I didn't want to go back to robbing and I couldn't get my boxing licence to become a professional boxer, but as one door closes another one opens, and if that meant putting my name to clubs, then so be it.

'So, who are these Maxwell Brothers?' I asked.

The owner explained how they came into his club every night, keeping the punters away and giving the place a bad reputation. I didn't want to know the ins and outs, we just agreed a price and the following night I went to the club tooled up.

I'm not one to huff and puff and growl at anyone but violence was my profession and I cared for no man. This club was now under my protection and I would kill any bastard who took a liberty.

The club was half empty when I walked in, the owner was nowhere to be seen. Straightaway I spotted the trouble-makers. They were standing at the bar. I took off my overcoat and put it over the back of a chair, and walked towards the Maxwells and introduced myself.

'Hello, boys, I'm Roy Shaw. Let me buy you a drink and I'll tell you how things are going to be from now on. You've had a good run at this club, now I'm running it. If you want to argue with that, now's your chance.'

Although I hadn't heard of the Maxwells, they must have heard about me because from then on they never returned to the club or gave me any trouble.

In actual fact, they turned out to be nice, respectful lads, but unfortunately I later heard they were charged with murder.

Word soon spread that I'd cleaned up the club in Dagenham, and in no time at all I was inundated with offers to put my name to clubs from Essex to London. One of the clubs I looked after in the West End was the kind of swish, up-market club where you could take a wife or girlfriend for a meal and a cabaret in relative safety.

All the chaps went there, 'faces' from all the firms, anyone who was anyone used to go there, including Freddie Foreman and Teddy Denis, men with reputations who were feared and respected. Everybody met there to discuss business, while leaving their girlfriends and wives chatting together.

It was a brilliant time for me. Everything had slotted into place better than I'd expected. After all that had gone on, at last I had found something that I enjoyed doing. Violence had always been a part of my life, but now I was getting paid for it and I loved it.

Every night was party night. I'd do my rounds of the clubs I looked after and planned it so I'd have a meal in one club, a drink in another, on to another to watch a cabaret, then another for more cabaret. It was party, party, all the way, and on top of that I was paid a wicked amount of money – what more could a man want?

New Year's Eve 1973 was the first Christmas and New Year I'd spent out of prison for 18 years and I wasn't going to miss one minute of it. I left home early that evening full of the festive spirit. I went straight to the A & R Club run by Ronnie Knight and Mickey Reagen and popped the cork off the first bottle of champagne for the evening. Then on to the Astor Club where everybody was happy. I felt I didn't have a care in the world, and by the time I reached the Embassy Club the pipers were piping in 1974.

Walking through the West End was an amazing experience and one that has never been equalled because it was the first New Year's Eve I'd been home in such a long while. The scenes were chaotic, the roads were jammed with traffic, horns blared and everyone was shouting and calling out 'Happy New Year' to each other.

The streets were packed with revellers shaking hands and kissing. I'd never witnessed anything like it before and was swept along with the occasion. Suddenly, a young woman kissed me full on the lips and slurred a Happy New Year wish, complete strangers shook my hand, patted my back and wished me well. Tears rolled down my face, I was so happy to be able to wish them the same.

There was only one thing missing in my life – a girlfriend. They say you never find anything if you look for it, and the one thing I wanted was someone to share my life with, and right out of the blue when I least expected it, I met the love of my life, Dorothy Tyler.

I was at a charity show, and I wasn't looking for love until Dorothy approached me and said hello. Bang. It was instant attraction – call it animal magnetism, call it what you like, but I called it love.

From that moment on, Dorothy and I were inseparable. I absolutely adored her and worshipped the ground she walked on, but we had one problem to overcome – she was married. I have never ever messed around with another man's wife or girlfriend before or since, but Dorothy was the exception to the rule. It wasn't a case of forbidden fruit tasting sweeter, that's bollocks. I found in Dorothy my friend, my lover and my soulmate.

Dorothy felt the same way as me and in no time at all decided to leave her husband. I knew she was giving up her beautiful home and stability for me. It was obvious she was apprehensive but I promised her everything would be all right, I wanted to make things perfect and to make her proud of me. I bought a plot of land and got permission to build a five-bedroom bungalow in Broxhill Road, Romford, Essex. We spent every hour building our bungalow, and while I worked on the building, Dorothy designed the interior. We were so happy together. I was the happiest I'd been in a long time. The house was more or less finished and was absolutely beautiful, it really was a labour of love.

For a while we were in seventh heaven. But – I hate to say it, there's always a but – unfortunately I wasn't ready to settle down, and I certainly wasn't ready for pipe and slippers, I still had a lot of partying and fighting to do.

I was offered the chance to earn a lot of quick and easy money. Wild, exaggerated sums were being bandied around. A old friend called Ronnie Smith came to see me and told me about a place called Barnet Fair where the gypsies meet once a year. He said it was a proper gypsy fair for horse trading, cock fighting and bare-knuckle fights, alongside coconut shies and penny arcades.

At first I wasn't interested in going, until Ronnie mentioned big money: £2,000 to be precise. Two grand is a lot of money to earn today, let alone back in 1974, and he reckoned I could earn it easily in an afternoon. Now that sort of money could come in handy, especially when you are building your own dream home. I needed a cash injection to boost my finances because buying the land and building the house had used up almost every penny I had, and it still wasn't quite finished. I didn't need any further thought and I told Ronnie to pick me up the next day.

Next morning, as arranged, Ronnie pulled up in his new white Mercedes. Dorothy had made me tea and toast for breakfast but there was no time so I grabbed a slice of toast, and with a final kiss on the cheek and a slap on her arse, I was gone.

We drove into the muddy fields of the gypsy fair and stuck out like sore thumbs. It was like stepping back five centuries to a medieval country fair. Snatches of conversation between men in boots and braces filled the air. They were spinning coins on odds and evens, yelling, 'Giss 'undred pound, boy. A fousand pound on Joe's Johnny.'

One man would bet against six or seven others on the turn of a coin while their sons rode bareback on heavy shire horses. Others looked on, bartering with the buyers who were saying, 'Look at dat, mate. Hair like dat. Tight mate. Black and white ...'

After each sale of a pony, the seller grabbed the buyer's hand, spat on his palm, slapping their hands together and said,

'Giv' me wot I said, mate. Giv' me a cockle back for luck.'

We parked the car and made our way through the crowd, looking for the bare-knuckle fights. We found between the chromed trailers a circle of men and made our challenge. There were countless takers, confident, loud, brash pikies, all brave amongst their own. I couldn't give a toss. I was there for the money, not the glory. Within no time at all, hundreds of pounds were placed in bets and the crowd swelled sensing an outsider about to have his arse kicked.

I took off my overcoat, jacket and shirt and gave them to Ronnie. The gypsy I was to fight stripped to the waist, unaware of what was in store. There were no preliminaries, no bells, just a baying mob. The fight was over in a matter of minutes and I won a grand.

I gave the grand to Ronnie and laid down the gauntlet for more challengers. A craggy-faced man with jet-black hair bragged about how good his son Elijah Boy was.

'You fight Elijah Boy next, he'll knock yer 'ead off.'

Bets were placed and Elijah Boy stripped to the waist. This fight lasted longer, in fact, we had a right old tear-up, but I won another grand and it went straight in Ronnie's pocket.

'Any more for any more?' I called.

There was one more challenger and one more loser. I won £3,000 that afternoon at Barnet Fair and the respect of the gypsies.

Unbeknown to me, in the crowd was Donny 'The Bull' Adams, King of the Gypsies, who was a teetotal, non-smoking, hard-faced mauler. I had come across him once before in prison and was well aware of his fearsome reputation. Donny 'The Bull' never challenged me that day, he just watched. However, within months, we were to fight literally for our lives. It was billed as a fight to the death between me and the King of the Gypsies. It was the biggest bare-knuckle fight ever staged and it was the fight that would change my life for good, one way or the other ...

CHAPTER 11

'TIL THE LAST DOG IS HUNG

'For three days before the fight I had stopped training to build up my energy and aggression. I was seething, fit to burst with cool, controlled ferocity ...'

Donny 'The Bull' Adams was no mug, his record proved that. In his long fighting career, he'd had 48 fights and 48 wins. Adams was a tough guy, a 15-stone, hard-faced mauler with a reputation that preceded him. He was well known and respected and would fight anyone who had the courage to go up against him. He fought mainly at gypsy horse fairs and anywhere else that big money was to be made.

I'd met up with Adams a couple of times before, once 20 years earlier in a boxing booth at a travelling fair and again in prison. On both occasions we took an instant dislike to each other. There was no reason for it, we just did. I didn't like him and he didn't like me – plain and simple. To me, he was just an animal and in the animal kingdom there is only one dominant male and instinctively that dominant animal's ego and pride will make him fight to survive, to protect, and to eat. Men are different; we don't need a reason or excuse to fight, we just do. And if it's to the death, then so be it.

Before I tell you about the fight between Adams and myself,

let me give you a little insight into the vicious, unruly, no-holds-barred world of unlicensed fighting. It's bare knuckle-fighting and means exactly that – fighting with your bare knuckles, raw, fiercely aggressive, street fighting. It's a barbaric sport of strength that has its roots in the 18th century. Unlicensed boxing has always flourished, rich with its own mythology of punch-drunk ex-pros, street-fighters, and amateur boxers under assumed names.

At boxing bouts, facilities were virtually non-existent. An area would be roped off in a field or sometimes on a wooden platform, and the aim was simply to knock your opponent senseless. A round ended only when one fighter fell to his knees battered and bleeding – after half a minute, half an hour, half a day, it didn't matter. It finished only when a man was down. Crowds baying for blood were controlled by 'beaters' – latter-day security men who were former fighters themselves, armed with whips, and often lived up to their name by beating back the excited crowds.

The first bare-fist champion was a fencer and duellist named James Figg, who held the title from 1719 to 1734. The last great bare-knuckle prize fight in England was between a Brit, Tom Sayers, and a Yank, John C Heenan, in April 1860. The fight was a gruelling battle and lasted two-and-a-half hours, and an astonishing 37 rounds, and only ended when the police stepped in, stopping the exhausted fighters from killing themselves.

It was soon after the fight that the Queensberry Rules were introduced. They were drawn up in 1867 and named after the Marquess of Queensberry, who took a keen interest in the sport. They were to become standards of proper behaviour in any fight, physical or verbal, and are still adhered to today.

Nowadays, it is against the law to hold a bare-knuckle fight or street fight as it is known, where there are no rules, no preliminaries, no standards, and no pleasantries, but these fights are still held and big money can be made at them.

I'd had a little taste of bare-knuckle fighting at Barnet Fair. I'd won £3,000 in an afternoon, quick and easy money if you had the bollocks for it.

The contest between me and Adams was billed as 'the fight of the century' and was to be a fight to the death. Joey Pyle took control. He organised everything from the venue to the tickets. To stage an unlicensed show on a large scale required a big venue but to hire a hall for an unlicensed fight was difficult, so we decided to stage the fight in the open air at a farm in Herefordshire.

More than one thousand £5 tickets were sold in London's East End for the fight which would have turned the sporting clock back 100 years. The contest, billed on the pink tickets as a fight to the death, sold like hot cakes, so Joey had a second batch printed which sold as quickly as the first thousand. Word on the street soon spread about the fight and inevitably reached the ears of the police.

In October 1975, Donny 'The Bull' and I landed in court in Hereford, and were bound over to keep the peace for one year. The main objection put forward by the police was that it was illegal for any boxer not to wear gloves, but the money from the sale of the tickets swayed us sufficiently to agree to wear lightweight gloves and to hold the match under the Queensberry Rules. In a word, we told them what they wanted to hear.

We left the court to a barrage of press, and the interest in the fight never wained. From then on, whenever I opened a newspaper there was a story about Donny Adams, King of the Gypsies. Headlines screamed out in the *Sunday Mirror* with Adams growling, 'Let me get at him.' It was 'Donny this ...', 'Donny that ...', blah, blah, blah.

I just kept myself to myself and said nothing. I reckoned actions speak louder than words. I didn't see Adams as a problem, just a way to earn money.

As boxing promoters go, Joey Pyle is the best, he's a silver-tongued, charismatic, dangerous fucker. He has the ability to hold everyone at arm's length, and you're only in Joey's company if you're invited. He's a good friend but a bad enemy. No problem is too big for Joey and he has the ability to minimalise any problem with just a word or the wave of his hand. In fact, I've never heard anyone say a bad word about Joey Pyle; wherever he goes he is well respected, but only a fool would take his kindness as a weakness.

The publicity for the fight cost Joey and the organisers diddly shit, the newspapers provided that. The media was in a frenzy. Adams and I were even asked to appear on *The Eamon Andrews Show* on television. Eamon asked us if the fight were to take place, whether we would actually fight to the death. For a moment there was a pause, but then, with no prompting, no hesitation, no umming or aahing there was just an unequivocal, chilling 'yes' from both of us.

It was the best advertisement we could have had because after the show we were inundated with offers of all sorts, including venues. Everybody wanted a piece of the action, from nightclubs to football pitches, but best of all Billy Smart offered us his big top circus tent at Winkfield, Berkshire.

It was perfect. Everything was arranged for 1 December 1975, and because of the television coverage and the interest, the price of the tickets doubled, and the amount of tickets sold exceeded our wildest expectations.

I trained hard but wherever I went I had an audience seeing how I shaped up, everybody wanting to know who the new kid on the block was, fresh out of prison, and did I really have what it took to kill a man with my bare hands? Is the Pope Catholic?

The hype had reached fever pitch, resulting in a film producer called Bob Brown coming to watch me spar. There was talk of a film deal and I admit I put on a show and showed off a bit by knocking out my sparring partners. Afterwards, the film producer said he was going to watch Adams spar to compare the two of us.

Later that night, I phoned Bob and asked him how Adams shaped up. He told me that Adams was very, very impressive. This made me think that maybe Adams was better than me and that planted a seed of doubt in my mind which made me train extra hard. I knew he was a bit of a tough nut and could bang, he had a reputation to prove it, but reputations are meant to be broken as easily as a lover's heart. Well, I was just that little Huckleberry to break his reputation.

Joey thought it was a good idea to have journalists watch me spar because Adams was attracting all the publicity and I was getting none. It's a well-known trait to give boxers nicknames, like Joe 'The Brown Bomber' Louis. Sonny Liston was nicknamed 'The Bear' because he was as big as a wild brown bear. It still goes on today, like Thomas 'The Hit Man' Hearns, so called because he literally destroys his opponents, and not forgetting 'Iron' Mike Tyson. Well, I was just little ol' Roy Shaw.

Out of the corner of my eye whilst sparring, I could see Joey and a group of journalists deep in conversation. I knew they were discussing publicity for the fight, when suddenly Joey threw his head back and roared with laughter.

'Do you want to tell him?' he asked one of the journalists.

I didn't know what they were talking about and, to be honest, I was too engrossed in what I was doing to care. The next morning I opened the newspaper and spread across two pages was my new nickname – Roy 'Pretty Boy' Shaw.

Joey later told me that it was a journalist from the *Sun* newspaper who had the bright idea to nickname me 'Pretty Boy' because he said I was a handsome devil. I didn't know if he was taking the piss or not, I've been called a lot of things in my time but pretty – never.

Finally, the long-awaited night of the fight arrived. On a rain-swept evening on the way to the venue, I sat in the back of a Mercedes deep in contemplation of what lay ahead. For three days before the fight I had stopped training to build up my energy and aggression. I was seething, fit to burst with cool, controlled ferocity.

The weather reflected my mood. It was a dark, stormy night, the wind howled through the trees, the sky was black and angry. Rain lashed against the car windows, the wiper blade squeaked as it dragged across the windscreen, making visibility nigh on impossible, but there was no mistaking the big top. Floodlights strobed across the sky, lighting up the tent and making it a huge showpiece.

Men battled against the elements to repair a gaping hole in the canvas that the wind had ripped apart. As we approached the entrance to the field, the whole area was cordoned off with ropes. Thick-set marshals directed the traffic into the parking areas while others collected tickets.

The driver's electric window glided halfway down, a drenched marshal stooped and growled, 'Gotcha tickets?'

'Roy Shaw,' the driver replied.

'Sorry, Mr Shaw,' the marshal said. 'If you would like to drive round the back of the tent everyone's waiting.'

I was shown into a makeshift dressing room, a place you would expect to be a sort of sanctuary for silent preparation, but mine was packed out with trainers and friends coming in and out to wish me good luck. I limbered up in the corner by rolling my head from side to side, loosening my neck muscles, and shadow boxed. I was keyed-up physically and mentally, nervous but filled with hate. I just wanted to get on with the fight, to get at Adams, to punch my hand through his body and rip his backbone out.

A warm-up fight was in progress. I could hear the roar of the crowd, you could almost smell the violence in the air. Joey Pyle came into the dressing room laughing and said, 'There's a right old tear-up going on out there. The ref has disqualified the fighters and you're on after the interval, Roy.'

The house lights went down. Adams was introduced. The pumping rock 'n' roll music engulfed the arena like a shroud. Adams had his own entourage with him. They sat ringside, hard, mean, pinched, white-faced men, waiting to explode.

Voices shouted in the darkness, 'COME ON, DONNY, FUCKING MURDER 'IM.'

The big top stank of lager, the air was filled with a nicotine smog, and a blood-thirsty crowd shouted and screamed, whipping themselves up into a frenzy.

The music pumped out from a sound system, a blaring,

slamming beat that rocked the big top, giving me my cue to enter. Security men stood in front of me as I made my way through the crowds. Groups of youngsters all dressed in Fred Perry and denims, with short-cropped hair, all pug-uglies and bar-room brawlers, chanted, 'Shaw-e ... Shaw-e ... Shaw-e ...'

I could tell the old fighters, not because of the puffy eyes and broken noses, but because they rose to the occasion in their suits and ties, embroidered with a certain dignity. Rough diamonds. You know the sort – do a lot for charity.

Adams stood in the ring in a gold silk dressing gown, pacing frantically around, oblivious and unsmiling. I climbed through the ropes to thunderous applause and smirked at Adams. He shrugged and fixed me with a savage stare.

Even before a fist was raised or a word spoken, a large brawny Irishman broke through security and into the ring, then bellowed that he wanted to fight us both. Adams and I grabbed him and slung him over the ropes. Security men grappled him to the floor and he was dragged, screaming and kicking from the big top.

The introductions started. The crowd were on their feet. Nosher Powell, the MC, a craggy-faced former stunt man whose claim to fame was a small part in a *Bond* film, introduced us both:

'Ladies and Gentlemen, the bout everybody has been waiting for. In the red corner, introducing Donny "The Bull" Adams, tipping the scales at 14st 6lb, fighting out of Waltham Cross, North London.'

Adams' followers gave out a rapturous cheer.

'And in the blue corner, introducing Roy "Pretty Boy" Shaw, weighing in at 15st 11lb from Dagenham, Essex.'

The referee motioned to me and Adams to go to the centre of the ring and said, 'I want you to touch gloves then please yourselves.'

I was exploding with energy as the bell went. Adams rushed at me. I hit him once on the chin with a right while he was standing up. Twice more on the chin while he was on one knee, and twice more while he was on the floor. Then I kicked him in the ribs and lifted him up so I could knock him down again. I was so pumped up with adrenalin and energy I really wanted to kill him. There was no count, just an uproar from the crowd. There was no finesse, no grace, just violence. The crowd hissed and spat as I jumped on Adams' head.

'HIT HIM DOWNSTAIRS, ROY. DOWNSTAIRS.'

'WHACK 'IM,' screamed a peroxide blonde as she leapt to her feet. 'JUST WHACK 'IM.'

Adams never got up. The referee and the marshals jumped into the ring and dragged me off him. My arm was raised by the referee as the winner.

My supporters were out of their seats, screaming for more, but Adams was down. His followers were swinging on the ropes urging him to get up but it was too late, the fight was over. The crowds were incensed, they didn't want the fight to finish. Scuffles broke out and a huge shiver of panic swept through the hall as if it was really going off at any moment. Then the lights were switched on and as suddenly as the violence arrived, it was gone, leaving only the crushed plastic glasses, the cigarette butts and the crowd pushing and shoving their way out of the tent, anxious to be away. In the dressing room, Adams' trainer wiped the blood away from his face with as much tenderness as a scorned woman.

I sat in the dressing room area with sawdust covering the floor and was joined by an embarrassed-looking Adams. He shook my hand and said it was a fair result. He looked around my dressing room at the men in wide-shouldered suits and dark glasses and said, 'Roy's the Guv'nor now. That makes him King of London.'

I admired Donny 'The Bull' Adams for that. It took a man, a real man, to shake me by the hand after I had just beaten him so savagely.

My purse for that fight was huge. I'm not about to divulge the amount, but we are talking telephone numbers, if that's not too vulgar. But ... and there's always a but. The man in charge of the parking facilities was a no-good pikey who owned a pub in Walthamstow. He was in charge of the money taken on the night from the parking, and it was estimated to be in excess of £6,000.

After the hullabaloo of the fight had died down, I met up with Adams and we both went to his pub to see 'Pikey the Stroke Puller' to get our money.

The 'Stroke Puller' asked us to join him in his office where he told us he had no money left. He said it had all gone on expenses. He had a couple of minders standing behind him which he thought would intimidate or frighten us. Adams said nothing and knew I was quite capable of dealing with the situation. At first I was polite, then I copped the needle and shouted, 'DON'T TAKE ME FOR A FUCKING MUG.'

I could see the cold indifference in his eyes, and it was a look I didn't like. I just had to wipe the arrogance away. I picked up an ashtray on his desk and smashed it into his head, busting his face wide open and splashing blood on to my new suit. His minders stepped back. I told the pikey I would go to his pub every night until he paid up all the dough he owed me. And I did just that. I got every penny back with interest and a new suit for luck, and the pikey pulled no more strokes – well, not on me anyway.

Now I had won the right to call myself the undisputed Guv'nor of London, and I would defend my title, whatever it took. I would fight absolutely anybody in the country as long as they had the money. I called the shots now and there was no way I was going to give up the title.

Challenges were few and far between but the lure of money beckoned its way across the Irish Sea to my next opponent, 'Mad Dog' Mullins, who had backers willing to stump up £20,000, which sounded good to me.

'Mad Dog' came with a good pedigree; he was an Irishman with a powerful reputation for knocking out tough guys throughout the Emerald Isle. Arrangements were made for a meeting at a pub in Notting Hill Gate between a 'Mad Dog' and an Englishman.

I waited in the bar but when 'Mad Dog' Mullins came in and introduced himself I was shocked. I had a Rottweiler bigger than him, he wasn't at all what I expected. Whoever gave him the

name 'Mad Dog' was either taking the piss or had a good sense
of humour. He looked more like a Jack Russell puppy skitting
about on a shiny wooden floor than a vicious, ferocious maniac
who wanted to take my title.

Everything was laid on by Joey Pyle at the Bloomsbury
Hotel, Russell Square, chosen because of the size of the
function room. For every fight I was involved in, part of the
proceeds were donated to charity. The charity sponsored at the
Bloomsbury Hotel was sending blind children to Russia to have
their eyesight restored.

The venue was packed out, the atmosphere was electric, and
support was overwhelming as Nosher Powell introduced us by
saying, 'Bring on the lions.' Everyone was out of their seats
cheering, and when the song by Gary Glitter blared out, 'Come
on, come on', the crowd stomped their feet and punched the air
in time to the music. The noise was deafening. I've never
experienced anything like it, I felt on top of the world.

Mullins was in the ring shadow boxing in my corner. I jumped
through the ropes and slung him out of the way. Ginger Ted, the
referee, stepped in to gain control but it was too late, I had
already beaten Mullins to the ground with the fiercest, fastest,
most accurate punches I had ever thrown. The fight was over
before it began. I looked over the ropes to Dorothy who was
sitting in the front row and winked.

Back in the dressing room, Mullins came to see me. I had to
take my hat off to him, he was a good sport because he was just
glad enough money was raised to send a pair of twins to Russia
to have their eyesight restored. But he made me laugh when he
said in his strong Irish brogue, 'Be Jaysus, Roy, I must be the
first Irishman to be knocked over the moon.'

I was riding high. I thought I was untouchable. I had won two
fights and I admit I enjoyed the adoration, the respect and the
crowds all shouting my name. I was King of London, king of the
hill, the big man on cloud nine with a pocket full of money and a
lady who loved me – Dorothy.

Our beautiful bungalow was nearly built. Both of us had

worked really hard on it and all credit to Dorothy, the interior was spectacular. Between us we had four big dogs: a Rottweiler, an Alsatian and two Great Danes.

Dorothy didn't want much to make her happy, and was satisfied with the simple things in life, like walking the dogs in the forest at the back of our land. Her idea of a good night out was for us to go out for a meal and hold hands, but at that stage in my life it was not my cup of tea. I had been locked up for a long time, and all I wanted to do was go out and do more bare-knuckle fighting. Looking back on it now, Dorothy helped me through all the hard times when I was scraping about for money while building the house. She stood by me and never complained once, but I was stupid, I had it all in the palm of my hand and ruined it.

One thing led to another, same old story, I just couldn't say no. They say money is the root of all evil; well, that's bollocks – it's women.

Women say all men are the same; we put our trousers on the same way, one leg at a time, and take them off the same way, whether the King of England who was forced to abdicate for the love of Mrs Simpson or the President of the United States and Monica Lewinsky. As far back as Adam and Eve, women shake their little *tushes* and men topple.

It doesn't matter how I try to paint it or use fancy words, the bottom line is – I cheated on Dorothy. It is the one regret I have in my life, and it's only now, way down deep in the hidden recesses of my mind, that I realise just how much I loved her, as sure as day follows night. Inevitably, Dorothy left me, but nowadays I can't help wondering how something so right could have gone so wrong and wherever she is now, I wish her health and happiness.

I jumped out of the frying pan and into the arms of the girl I was playing around with – Sharon Mitchell. She moved in with me and for a while we were happy but it wasn't to last. I liked her but I didn't love her. However, she's still my friend today, it was a shame we didn't click.

I'd got what I thought I wanted – the freedom to go out, do as I pleased, and answer to no one. My unlicensed boxing career really took off. I was hot, so hot I was sizzling. Joey Pyle put on some really good shows and I was making money hand over fist. I fought another couple of fighters, one called Mickey Glaxted from the East End – a right mongrel in my opinion. I beat him in three rounds. It was stopped because he was taking too much punishment. Next was Terry Hollingsworth, the ABA champion. I trained hard for that fight but Hollingsworth was finished in the first round.

I had built up a reputation for myself and quite a following. I had many well-wishers and even received a telegram from none other than the greatest boxer who ever lived – Muhammad Ali. Angelo Dundee, Ali's trainer in Miami, wrote to Alex Steene, who was my manager, saying, 'I hear you are handling "Pretty Boy" Shaw. Ali is definitely interested in meeting "Pretty Boy", as there is no room in this world for two pretty faces. If at all possible, he would like to meet him, the sooner the better.'

There was no better accolade a man could receive. Unfortunately, I never did get to meet the man I admire most, Muhammad Ali, let alone fight him. But there was one man who I was to meet right out of the blue when a pal of mine who was running a pub in Hoxton came to see me. He was at his wit's end because he had trouble in his pub. He started to tell me about his problem.

'The geezer's a fucking nuisance, Roy,' he said. 'When I call time he just refuses to leave. He's taking right liberties. Get rid of him for me, please, Roy.'

I agreed to go to his pub and sort out his little problem. The name of the little problem ... Lenny McLean.

CHAPTER 12

RUMOURS AND REPUTATIONS – MCLEAN V. SHAW

'I kept on smashing into his ribs, and each time he flinched and recoiled from every violent thrust. He fell on to the ropes twice, but managed to get up on the count of three, but it was too late, I knew I had him as long as I kept the pressure up. I hit him hard in the stomach for the final time sending him reeling backwards on to the ropes ...'

O N THE FRONT COVER of Lenny McLean's book *The Guv'nor*, he says about himself, 'I look what I am, a hard bastard!' and make no mistake, he was just that. He was everything anyone expected a gangster, a tough guy or a fighter to be, he epitomised them all. It's difficult for me to talk about Lenny McLean as he has recently died; in fact, I started writing this book on the very day he was buried. I was invited to the funeral but I declined.

I decided not to go, first out of respect for his widow, Val, and his children, Jamie and Kelly; and second, I'm no hypocrite. If I had attended the funeral I would have been just that. By going, it would have indicated that I liked him and I didn't. It's no secret that Lenny and I were arch enemies. Lenny was everything I'm not. He was larger than life, up-front, and in your face, whereas I'm more reserved, never been one for the limelight, always kept low-key, and a loner.

But I'm taking nothing away from Lenny McLean; he was a big, powerful man. He was huge, the size of a house, and could instil the fear of Christ in many a man's heart with just a look. I might be leaving myself wide open to criticism here, but I don't give a toss, I'm going to say it as it was – please or offend.

There will be those who say, foolishly, that I can say these things now because Lenny's not here to defend himself, but Lenny would have been the first to admit that if I had anything to say, I would say it to his face. Bearing in mind I'm choosing my words carefully, not because I'm bothered for one minute what anyone would say or think of me, but it's not right to speak ill of the dead, and I wouldn't disrespect his family by doing so, I've just told the truth because the truth is much simpler.

The first time I heard Lenny McLean's name was when a pal told me he was causing a problem in his pub in Hoxton. I assured my mate I would sort the problem out by going to the pub and having a word with the guy causing all the trouble. But the night I went, Lenny wasn't there, and word on the street soon spread that I was looking for him. After that, the name McLean kept cropping up in conversation. I'd heard rumours about his reputation, that he'd knocked out some tough men in the East End. Mention Lenny McLean's name and everyone's reaction was the same: a nod of the head, and 'Whoah ... keep movin'.'

They all said the same; he's awesome, he's a size, he's this, he's that. So fucking what if he's big? The size of him didn't bother me diddly-squat; the bigger they come, the harder they fall.

So when the money was laid on the table to have a bare-knuckle fight with Lenny, it didn't come as a great surprise to me because this town, London town, wasn't big enough for the both of us. I agreed to fight him on the understanding that it was winner takes all.

The venue was Sinantra's nightclub in Croydon. It was packed to the rafters with supporters, both mine and Lenny's and a few who sat on the fence. Lenny had claimed in the newspapers that he was going to rip my head off and everyone had come to see him try. Until the night, I still hadn't even laid eyes on McLean.

The atmosphere in the hall was charged, the music boomed out full blast from the sound system, and I'd already run the gauntlet and was in the ring having my hands bandaged when McLean climbed through the ropes. I whispered to my corner, 'Fucking size of him!'

McLean's trainer was struggling to get the gloves on Lenny because his hands were so big they didn't fit. They even had to send out to the dressing room to get a bigger pair. The delay made me anxious. I was thinking to myself how much I wanted to get at him and hurt him. The MC was again Nosher Powell. He introduced me as the hardest man in England – challenger Lenny McLean.

The bell rang indicating the start of the first round. I decided to steam heavily into McLean's belly because he was so tall I knew it would double him up. I hit him with some lovely body shots. Then McLean spouted off to the crowds, 'Look, he can't hurt me.' I stuck one on his chin which soon shut him up, then carried on punching him in the belly to weaken him. By the end of the first round, he was puffing when he staggered back to his corner. I was excited at the wild joy of my own vitality.

In round two, by constantly attacking and shoving McLean on to the ropes, I shaped the fight and gave it momentum. I was switching blows from his belly to his chin. McLean never laid a glove on me but I was wearing myself out punching him. At the end of the second round, I was the one puffing.

I took a large gulp of cold water from a plastic bottle, rinsed my mouth out and spat into a metal bucket. Nosher Powell and the famous actor Gene Hackman, who played the character Popeye Doyle in the film *The French Connection*, who'd come to see me fight, shouted to me to have a rest.

'Let him do some work, Roy,' they yelled.

The bell went for round three. I only knew one way to fight – forward. I tracked McLean round the ring like a fox on a hunt, but there was nowhere for him to run and nowhere to hide, I was all over him like a rash. I banged him with a right but he had a rock solid chin. McLean was fighting now with desperation, ignoring the blood – his blood. I smashed a right to his head, he staggered along one side of the ring. I swung a wide left and a right that wobbled him. He hung on to the ropes and through gritted teeth hissed, 'I've had enough.'

McLean was demoralised, weary and bleeding after my savage attack. He looked to the referee to intervene but I could taste victory. With one final clubbing right hand to the head, the referee stepped in and raised my arm in victory.

Usually the purse for a fight is divided, but McLean earned nothing for that fight, not one penny, that was the condition I fought him. It was winner takes all and the purse was good.

My next fight was at Alexandra Palace. It was against Ron Stander, who'd fought for the World Title against Joe Frazier in Las Vegas. The actor Gene Hackman and a friend of his, another actor Jack O'Hallanon, who'd starred in a few *Bond* films, arranged the fight after watching me beat McLean.

Stander was a true professional, and had gone the distance with some of America's best boxers. I knew I had a tough fight on my hands and trained hard. To me, this was an opportunity to show what I could do, not just in England but in America, too.

Ron Stander flew into London asking, 'Who the fuck is "Pretty Boy" Shaw?' He'd never heard of me in the States, and it was obvious he didn't take the fight with me seriously. To him, I was just a way of earning a quick buck. He thought he could breeze into England and beat me, then breeze out with a pocketful of money. The main reason was that he'd seen how our heavyweights performed in America, which wasn't very well. At that time, our great white hope was Joe Bugner, who lasted the distance with Ali and was disliked by the British public for beating Henry Cooper, affectionately known as Our 'Enery.

Terry Downs picked up Stander and his entourage from the

airport and then took him out on the town for a good time. He wasn't concerned in the slightest about coming to a strange country to fight, he just laughed at the mere mention of my name.

Stander didn't bother training, because he thought I wasn't a problem and when he was in the gym he joked around by kicking a punch bag and mimicking Ali saying, 'London Bridge is falling down, and so will "Pretty Boy" in London town.'

It was while he was joking about that he tripped and fell over, cracking his ribs. I was unaware of this at the time. On the night of the fight, I stood toe to toe with Stander in the middle of the ring. I wanted to look good to show what I could do. There were many important people in the audience from the boxing world and it meant a lot to me to win.

I punched Ron Stander harder than I have ever hit anyone in my life, with good clean punches connecting with his chin each time. It didn't matter what I threw at him. I couldn't hurt him. He just laughed. He was talking to me through his gum shield saying, 'Come on, boy, keep it up.' I couldn't believe it, I was hitting him as hard as I could and getting nowhere. He kept on saying, 'Keep it going, keep it going.' He soaked up every punch like a giant sponge. I think he was just trying to tire me out. Then I switched tactics and sank a crushing right into his rib cage. At last I had hurt him, he moaned and winced. I thought, Great, at last I was doing some damage.

I kept on smashing into his ribs, and each time he flinched and recoiled from every violent thrust. He fell on to the ropes twice, but managed to get up on the count of three, but it was too late, I knew I had him as long as I kept the pressure up. I hit him hard in the stomach for the final time sending him reeling backwards on to the ropes.

The referee stepped between us and started counting, ' ... Seven ... eight ... nine ... ten,' and with a wave of his hands the ref counted Stander out.

My arm was raised in victory. But I'm not taking anything away from Ron Stander and I'm sensible enough to know that if he hadn't hurt his ribs before the fight, he would have mullered me – no question about it.

After a fight in the bare-knuckle world of boxing, it's normal for would-be challengers to challenge the winner. After the Stander fight, Lenny McLean jumped into the ring and challenged me for a return. McLean had had a couple of fights since ours. He'd fought and lost against a fella called Cliff Fields who was a true full-blooded heavyweight professional. He'd also fought and lost against a man called Johnny Waldren. Waldren was a six-foot tall, dark, good-looking amateur fighter and no mug. In fact, he had fought McLean and knocked him out twice in the first round which was something I never managed to do. Waldren had had a return match with McLean and, again, knocked him out.

After I beat Stander, McLean kept challenging me for a return fight, and eventually I agreed and the return was scheduled at the Rainbow Rooms. But I'd become lazy, a fat-cat, I'd earned more money than I could spend and was just going through the motions. Looking back on it now, I must have been mad; I was in my early forties and, like most boxers, I should have given it up while I was on top, but I've got to say I didn't know when to quit. Up until that point, I had an unbeaten record and should have realised that I was fighting a man 12 years younger, six inches taller and four stone heavier when there was really no need.

I had nothing to prove by fighting McLean a second time. I had beaten him once, but agreed to fight him again. Just for the hell of it.

I made no preparations for the fight, I didn't change my diet or do any extra training. I had been taking capsules of ginseng, a plant from the Far East, whose roots are believed to increase energy and stamina. On the way to the venue, I stopped at a Chinese herbalist and bought a bottle of liquid ginseng. I had never taken it before in liquid form and wasn't aware of its potency.

I sat in the back of the car and drank half the bottle thinking it would give me a boost but it worked in reverse. I became sluggish and lethargic, and the only way to describe how I felt was as if I had been smoking cannabis. It was a strange feeling, I was aware of everything going on around me, the loud music, the roaring crowds, my corner giving me instructions but everything was in slow motion. I climbed into the ring in a daze, as weak as a kitten. The ginseng has taken away all my strength, and now I knew how Samson felt when Delilah cut off his hair. I was so chilled out when the bell rang and McLean came at me like a charging bull, he knocked me down within minutes. It was as easy as taking candy from a baby. I couldn't comprehend why I was so slow. I'd lost the fight and there was nothing I could do about it and like many fighters before me I had to know how to lose with grace and dignity.

Life is a learning process that never ends. What you make of your life is up to you, all the answers lie within you, because you know yourself best. McLean hadn't hurt me physically, but had dented my pride and taken away my title. I had learnt a lesson that night; nobody, including me, is indestructable.

After the fight, I was now the one challenging McLean for a return. I even challenged him on Gary Bushel's TV show in front of millions of viewers, but he refused.

I had another three fights, one with a man by the name of Kevin Paddock, who'd fought and beaten McLean on points. The fight went eight rounds and I beat him no problem.

My next fight was with Harry Starbuck who had a fearsome reputation and believe me, he'd earned it. He'd had 14 fights and 14 knock-outs. I liked him, he's one of the old school, a man of respect who shook my hand after I beat him.

I didn't know it at the time but my last ever fight was with a man called Lou Yates at Ilford. He was a well-known fighter, well respected but posed no problem as I stopped him in the second round. At the end of the fight, I challenged McLean again for a return, but again he refused. I never did have that return fight with Lenny McLean, and he took my title as the Guv'nor of London to the grave with him. I'm not taking anything away from him – he won the title fair and square. At the end of his autobiography Lenny says, 'Some days get imprinted on your mind more than others. Meeting my wife Val ... the births of my Jamie and Kelly ... and beating Roy Shaw.'

To me, Lenny McLean was just one in a long line of men I fought throughout my life. No more, no less. So when I read his book I was touched by his words. I never knew that beating me meant so much to him, so perhaps it was only right that he died still holding the title of The Guv'nor.

CHAPTER 13

THE DEVIL DANCES IN AN EMPTY POCKET

'Violence has been my friend and companion for the whole of my life, it never turned its back on me, never betrayed me, and it never let me down ...'

I MIGHT HAVE LOST MY TITLE AS THE THE GUV'NOR to Lenny McLean in the boxing ring, but outside the world of unlicensed fighting, my life was beginning to change for the better. Although I didn't realise it at the time, it seemed I had the Midas touch, but unlike the Greek legend I've never prayed to be relieved of the gift of everything I touch turning to gold.

I have always avoided discussing what I earned from whatever deals I've been involved in. Maybe I was in the right place at the right time, or I just had some good fortune. Call it luck, call it what you like, I call it using my loaf. I admit I earned a fortune in the ring, albeit an unlicensed ring, but I was sensible enough to invest my money wisely which enabled me to diversify. I was a street fighter who took on the role of a successful respectable businessman with ease.

At this time in my life, I had fingers in many pies. Boxing was no longer the be-all and end-all of my life. I've always been one for careful planning with my finances and I am a great believer in speculating to accumulate. I had no intention of going back to my old ways ever again, but obviously you can't do much without money. When you are potless, the temptation to get on the wrong side of the law is far greater because the devil dances in an empty pocket. Take it from me, there is no such thing as the perfect crime. It doesn't matter who you are, inevitably you end up in prison. I know – I was that soldier, or should I say convict, but that's all water under the bridge now and I never intend to paddle in those waters again.

I set my goals high, I wanted to achieve what everyone else does – health, wealth and happiness. I had my health, I found my happiness in freedom, all that was left was wealth. So that was my goal.

I was already comfortably off, but there is no such thing as having too much money. The house that Dorothy and I built together was finished, but I had lost Dorothy and there were too many memories for me to stay. I put the house on the market and doubled my money. This made me think that perhaps buying and selling property could be my future. There was nothing like earning an honest pound and it felt good that I no longer had to keep looking over my shoulder.

Just by chance, by a sheer fluke, I came across a mansion in Upminster called Cranham Court, a former nursing home that had gone bankrupt. It had a long tree-lined drive with colourful rhododendron bushes on either side, emerging into spectacular grounds surrounding an imposing house that literally took your breath away. From the moment I saw it, I wanted it.

I pulled out all the stops until I had the keys to my own mansion in my sticky paws. In a matter of months, I had swapped the title of Guv'nor of London for Lord of the Manor.

I lived in Cranham Court for two years while I renovated it from top to bottom, but from the onset I bought it purely as an investment, and a bloody good investment it was, too. When I sold the mansion I tripled my money. It didn't matter what I did, it seemed everything I touched turned to gold.

They say life begins at 40 and it's true. I was riding along on the crest of a wave, everything was perfect, but just when I thought it was safe to come out of the water I foolishly let my guard slip for a moment. The incident that landed me back in prison was all stuff and nonsense and, I'm loath to say, was something as simple as road rage.

The phrase 'road rage' is a relatively new term, used to describe the blind fury that can overtake a driver, male or female, who in other circumstances may well be a calm, reasonable individual. But when behind the wheel of a car, he or she turns into an ignorant, arrogant, abusive maniac. If you drive a car, then at one time or another you've been involved in road rage. Men who are normally gentlemen, myself included, holler obscenities at whoever gets in the way, women included. I've said to myself a hundred times 'fucking women drivers', and school runs are the worst. When mothers collect their children they're not concentrating on driving, their minds are full of fish fingers and chips for tea, ballet classes, swimming lessons, and it's starting to rain and the washing's still out! It's as if they are blinkered; they stop where they like, park where they like, totally oblivious to other drivers. In everyday life, men wouldn't dream of verbally attacking a woman with a torrent of rude insults, but once they get behind the wheel of a car all pleasantries go out of the window. They no longer see these drivers as women, they don't care whether they are old or young, they blast their horns and wave clenched fists out of the window shouting: 'Move it, you slag. Are you fucking blind?'

Women are the same though. Once behind the wheel of a car, they're no longer delicate little flowers. I've been on the receiving end of a woman's tongue, and they can be vicious little vixens. Try reversing into their space in a supermarket car park, then you'll be sorry.

But the real danger is when it's man against man, when neither will give in. A simple gesture can lead to a complete character change and turn an ordinary Joe into Damon Hill and the chase begins. Drivers can be completely devoid of any reason. They don't care that they have the baby strapped in the back seat, or that their pregnant wife is sitting next to them. They're going to catch that son-of-a-bitch who called them a wanker and when they do, they're gonna ... they're gonna ... That's the problem, they're not really sure what they'll do when, or if, they catch them. Nine times out of ten the incident fizzles away to nothing, but unfortunately for the son-of-a-bitch who called me a wanker, I caught him, and when he got out of his car still spitting obscenities at me, I had no alternative but to rip his face off.

I was sentenced to six months' imprisonment and was taken directly to Pentonville jail. It had been nearly 15 years since I'd been inside. The only thing that had changed was the overcrowding, and that meant only one thing, more aggression.

I'd forgotten what it was like in prison. It's a human cesspit full of depraved degradation where anything goes. From the moment I walked into Pentonville, I had an overwhelming gut reaction of revulsion, it was an instant onslaught on my senses. Prison has its own distinctive noises, blaring radios, men shouting, doors slamming, keys jangling.

The smell, that putrid smell that only a prison has of urine, shit and body odour all rolled into one. You can almost taste prison. I wanted someone to slap the bad taste out of my mouth and bring me to my senses. I felt I had taken a step back 15 years. It stirred feelings inside me that I'd much rather have forgotten, feelings of anger and hatred and a burning desire to hurt someone, anyone, totally consumed me.

I was taken to a cell containing two other prisoners. I stood in the doorway and looked. There was no way I was stepping one foot inside that overcrowded shit hole. I shook my head and told the screw to forget it, I wanted a single cell. He laughed. He fucking laughed and said nobody has a single cell nowadays. It must have been the look on my face or the hate in my eyes that persuaded him to reconsider.

'You'll have to see the doctor,' he said as he averted his eyes from my gaze.

I walked into the doctor's office adamant that I was not willing to share a cell with others. The doctor was sensible enough to listen to me. I didn't beat about the bush, I just told him how it was and said, 'I've killed before, and if I'm put into a cell with anyone else, believe me I will kill again, and you will be responsible.'

The doctor thumbed through my prison record. As he read the contents, I could almost hear his mind working overtime. He read of the violence that I had inflicted, the stabbings, and of the cut-throat world in which I'd lived for so long. He read reports of my mental condition, of my stay in Broadmoor, and of my determination not to be broken.

How I was a psychopath, a madman, a maniac, a nutter, it was all in that report, even the 'murder' of Mr Brown in Parkhurst, and it made colourful reading. He closed my file and looked into my eyes. The decision lay with the doctor. It could so easily have gone either way. Throughout my life, it has been a knock-on effect, with one violent incident leading to another. If the doctor had said I had to share a cell, I would have had no hesitation, none whatsoever, in carrying out my threat to kill, then who knows what would have happened to me? Maybe I would still be in prison today or, worse still, back in the dungeons in Broadmoor.

As I sat in my single cell I had six months to reflect. Looking back, I had wasted so much time in prison, it dawned on me that I was on the wrong side of 40 to waste any more years. There and then, sitting on that prison bunk in Pentonville, I made the conscious decision that I would never return to prison, and up until now – touch wood – I haven't.

*   *   *

I didn't know I was looking for love until I found it in the guise of my second wife Patsy in the Royal Oak pub in Loughton, Essex. Women have never played a major part in my life. Sure, I like women, what man doesn't? But I've never needed or relied on anyone, least of all a woman. Maybe I'm being cynical, but you really can't trust anyone but yourself. Women can be a man's Achilles heel, the one weak spot that could finally bring a man to his knees. I'd felt vulnerable only once before during my stay in Broadmoor when Carolina, my wife, left me for another man and I didn't like that feeling one bit. Since then I could take them or leave them. I don't know if it is a good or bad thing, it's how I've learned to protect my emotions.

Although I am very much a man's man, I'm very self-sufficient. I do my own cooking, cleaning, washing and ironing, I've never needed a woman to do these things for me. I've never had the luxury of being pampered or spoilt in my life. After saying all this, in the words from the musical, 'There is nothing like a dame, nothing in this world ...' and when I laid eyes on Patsy, I was caught, hook, line and sinker.

She was beautiful, I couldn't take my eyes off her all evening, but I wasn't about to make myself look a fool by approaching her. It was blatantly obvious to me and everyone else around that she was interested, but I believe in everything coming to he who waits, and by the end of the evening she had introduced herself and we shared a cab home to her place. I liked Patsy, I liked her a lot, and one look at that face and my heart fluttered. When I asked her out for a date and she accepted I was thrilled.

We had a whirlwind romance – I loved having a beautiful woman on my arm and I delighted in spoiling her. I had all the time and money in the world to devote to her, and after a few months I asked her to marry me and she accepted.

We had some lovely times together. I could relax with Patsy. She was good fun to be with. I'd take her out to see a show or for dinner. They were idyllic times.

I was happy, truly happy. I gave Patsy *carte blanche* to buy what she wanted. If she was happy, I was happy. Up until that point, Patsy hadn't witnessed my explosive temper. She'd heard rumours that I was a bit of a rascal, but she hadn't actually seen it first-hand until we went to pick up her wedding dress in Romford, Essex. Parking in the town was difficult but luckily I spotted a space and prepared to reverse back into it. While I manoeuvred my Bentley, to my annoyance someone drove into my space.

I jumped out of my car and told him that it was my space and to fuck off, but he wouldn't have it, he was going to park there and that was that. Now I was absolutely livid, it was like showing a red rag to a bull. I opened his car door and pulled him out. There was no reasoning with me and no stopping me, I forgot all about Patsy and her wedding dress and the nice things in life. For a moment I had the old familiar adrenalin rush. Anger can be like an old friend, it never lets me down. I hit the driver so hard that he fell back into his car, and he lashed back by kicking me in the chest. I grabbed hold of his legs and smashed his car door on them until Patsy screamed hysterically, and it was only those screams that brought me back to my senses. I suppose it took the shine off collecting her wedding dress somewhat.

The Old Bill arrived and I was carted off to the police station for assault. Give Patsy her due, she used her head and explained that it wasn't my fault. On the other hand, the cocky little fucker who'd caused all the trouble in the first place didn't press charges, and to cut a long story short I was released without charge. Unbeknown to me, the incident had caused more trouble than I realised.

Three days later, my home was raided by the drug squad. Questions had been asked as to how I made my money, and the police thought there had to be a sinister way I could afford a Bentley, a beautiful bird and a big gaff out in the woods. They reasoned it couldn't be legitimate, it just couldn't, a known villain who had spent the best part of his life inside having it all. But they were wrong. So wrong. They left no stone unturned when they raided my house looking for drugs, guns, bodies – whatever it was they were looking for, they didn't find it, try as they might.

I held my head high because much to their dismay I'm clean and I have been for years. Everything I have is bought and paid for legitimately and I'm proud to be able to say that, so fuck 'em.

I married Patsy and had a wonderful wedding reception at Epping Forest Country Club and honeymooned on the Orient

Express, then on to a cruise stopping at breath-taking places like Venice and Hawaii. In fact, we travelled all round the world together. It was fabulous, but almost instantly I realised I'd made a mistake. Patsy was beautiful, there are no two ways about that, she was everything a man could ask for. But ... but ... but ... There's no fucking buts about it – I just fell out of love, plain and simple. I met her, married her, took her around the world and divorced her, all in three years.

I'm sure that the road rage incident that happened three years earlier opened a can of worms. The police remained convinced that I was something I wasn't – a drug dealer or an arms dealer – whatever, it was decided come rain or shine, I just had to be up to no good.

My house had been spun a few times by the drugs squad and each time they found nothing because there was nothing there. They couldn't get it into their heads that I was clean and, try as they might, they couldn't prove otherwise. It rattled their cage. I knew they were out to pin something on me and I wasn't being paranoid because I was told the Old Bill were sniffing around asking questions about me. They even went to clubs and pubs around the area warning the owners, bouncers and managers, saying I was trouble.

I know this for a fact, having got it straight from the horse's mouth, because they went to a mate's pub called the Spencers Arms in Hornchurch and did just that – said I was trouble.

A short time later, a club opened in Romford, a fashionable, up-market night spot. The opening night was by invitation only for VIPs and celebrities. I was invited and spent the evening in the VIP lounge sipping champagne with the owner. It was a good night, there was no trouble, no incident, nothing. A week later, I returned to the club with a lady on my arm but, to my surprise, there was no welcome, and we were greeted with a complete change of attitude. It was no longer 'Welcome to my club, Mr Shaw ... Sit in the VIP lounge, Mr Shaw ... Drink champagne on the house, Mr Shaw'. Instead, it was a case of 'You ain't coming in'. Well, what the fuck happened to warrant a complete turnaround in a week? The reason had to be that the Old Bill had paid them a little visit.

I was taken aback and asked to see the owner. I'd been left standing in the foyer of the nightclub arguing the toss as to whether or not I was going to be allowed in. I don't like arguing and I don't like being mugged off, full stop. I tried to be reasonable. One minute I'm in the club drinking champagne with the owner, and the next I'm getting grief from the bouncers – from the *bouncers* of all things! I'd been doing their job before they were even born. They puffed out their chests and gave it 'the big-I-am', feeling brave because there were a few of them. There is always safety in numbers.

Well, I've never needed anyone, there was only ever just me and if they thought they were hard enough then I was more than willing and able to take them on one at a time, and told them exactly that. Sensing it was all about to go off, I told the lady to go and sit in a cab outside. Once she was safely out of the way I didn't argue any further with the doormen, I just knocked the nearest one out. Not one of them was a real man prepared to stand toe to toe with me, instead they jumped me.

Whenever I've fought in the past, I've never felt pain. It must be the adrenalin that anaesthetizes me, but on this occasion one of the bouncers, a big nasty bastard, hit me with something on the head as he sneered, 'All the time Shaw is vertical he is dangerous.'

He hit me maybe three or four times so hard it almost knocked me senseless. I don't know what he struck me with, but whatever it was, it fucking hurt.

By now the fight had moved outside the club. I fought like a wild cat but there were just too many bouncers for one man to handle alone. There was one in particular, the nasty bastard who kept hitting me on the head, who was a bully and took full advantage of the situation I was in, and used the opportunity to try and knock me horizontal. Well, that wasn't going to happen. They would have had to kill me to stop me. I fought like a madman and pushed them back towards the entrance. As one bouncer ran inside so another followed. None of them wanted to fight me one to one, and before I knew it they were all inside with the doors safely locked behind them.

I was as mad as hell and went back to the entrance of the club. The bouncers stood behind the locked glass doors. I didn't shout or make a song and dance about what happened, I just tapped on the glass and warned them, 'I'll be back.'

I got in the cab and took the lady home, then collected a hammer from my garage and returned to the club. Outside in the car park was a brick-built dustbin shed where I hid, waiting for the club to empty.

By 2.00am the clubbers started to leave, and one of the doorman must have spotted me as he pointed in my direction. I stayed where I was but it wasn't long before the Old Bill arrived. One of the police turned his headlights on to the dustbin shed and I was caught in the light like a rabbit in the night. I threw my hammer in a dustbin and stood up. The police grabbed me and searched me, asking me what I was doing. I told them nothing.

I was escorted off the premises. As I walked past the doormen, I smiled, pointed and whispered to each one of them in turn, 'I'm gonna do you. I'm gonna do you.' And as I reached the one who had been hitting me over the head, I said, 'But especially, I'm gonna do you.'

I thought long and hard about what had happened at the nightclub. The incident stuck in my throat, I tried to let it go but I couldn't. I had two choices: the first was to forget all about it and do nothing; and the second was to take care of it, and take care of it properly. If I decided to take the first choice I knew that it would only be a matter of time before I had every little shit in the area trying to take a liberty, and that means everything I have ever stood for and everything I have ever believed in meant nothing.

From as far back as I can remember, I've stood up for what I believed in; from the bullies in the playground, the Sergeants in the Army, the vindictive bastards in prison, Broadmoor, and in the boxing ring, I've bowed down to no man. If I took my second choice to take care of the situation I'd keep my pride and my dignity, even if that meant spending the rest of my days behind bars. There was no contest. I've never walked away from a fight in my life and I wasn't about to start now.

I couldn't do all the doormen, that just wasn't feasible. But there was one, the nasty bully boy who'd tried to take advantage of me. I found out where he lived, the evenings he worked and the times he finished.

As I stood alone, lurking in the shadows at the top of the lane where he lived, I no longer felt angry, I felt no sorrow, no pity and I certainly felt no fear. The funny thing is, at that moment it dawned on me – I liked violence. When I sought retribution for whatever reason, I wasn't sure if it was the power I enjoyed or if I just liked to see the fear in the other man's eyes. Whatever it is, violence has been my friend and companion for the whole of my life, it never turned its back on me, never betrayed me, and it never let me down.

As I stood in the shadows in the early hours of that morning waiting to seek my revenge, I looked up at the clear night sky and at the stars and at the full moon and sighed. At that moment I became at one with myself. I thought back over my life, back to my schooldays in the playground and the bullies.

I hated those boys for what they did to me, but if I was to meet them today I would shake their hands and thank them because it was them who made me strong and the person I am today.

It was then and there that I felt able to admit to myself that I was actually going to enjoy making an example of the doorman and would take great pleasure in what I was about to do ...

And may the Lord have mercy on his soul ...

BOXING MEMENTOES

MUHAMMAD ALI
says:
"THERE'S ONLY ROOM FOR ONE PRETTY BOY IN THE BOXING WORLD"

ROY "PRETTY BOY" SHAW
says:
"THATS RIGHT... AND I'M THE ONE"

ROY "PRETTY BOY" SHAW CHALLENGES MUHAMMAD ALI TO A FIGHT TO THE FINISH, NO HOLDS BARRED, ANY TIME, ANY PLACE.

ALEX STEENE (right) is willing to co-promote a bout between ROY SHAW and MUHAMMAD ALI anywhere in the world.

WANTED

JOE BUGNER

TO MEET

ROY SHAW

REWARD: £50,000

Obtainable from

JOEY PYLE   and   **ALEX STEENE**

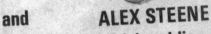

for the right to stage the fight the British public want to see

In the clearing stands a boxer
And a fighter by his trade
And he carries a reminder
of every cut that's laid him out
or cut him 'til he cried out
In his anger and his pain
'I am leaving, I am leaving'
But the fighter still remains ...

Excerpt from The Boxer
by Simon and Garfunkel

BUY ROY SHAW UNLEASHED, THE BESTSELLER BY THE ULTIMATE HARDMAN!

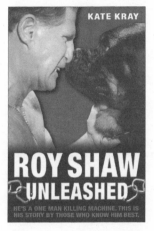

KATE KRAY

ROY SHAW
UNLEASHED

HE'S A ONE MAN KILLING MACHINE. THIS IS HIS STORY BY THOSE WHO KNOW HIM BEST.

When Kate Kray wrote *Pretty Boy*, she interviewed scores of people. Almost without exception, as she was leaving, they would say to her, 'I'll tell you something about Roy – but don't tell him I told you...'
These stories were too shocking and close to the bone to include without Roy's permission – now that permission has been granted. The result is genuinely blood-curdling.
Roy Shaw: Unleashed is a collection of those stories, as told by Roy himself and those close to him. True stories of murder and violence; the final truth about his famous fights with Lenny 'The Guv'nor' McLean; incredible tales from inside the shadowy criminal fraternity from the likes of Mad Frankie Fraser and the Richardsons. It also reveals a gentler side to this relentless fighting machine as Kate searches for the one thing that will make Roy's intriguing life complete – the lost love who has eluded him for the last twenty years...

OUT IN PAPERBACK AT £7.99

Prices include postage and packing in the UK. Overseas and Eire, add £2.00.
To order by credit card, telephone 0207 3810666.
Alternatively, send a cheque or postal order with your name and address to:
John Blake Publishing, 3 Bramber Court, 2 Bramber Road, London, W14 9PB

ROY SHAW was born in Stepney in 1936. In 1963 he was sentenced to 18 years for a record-breaking armed robbery.

He started bare-knuckle fighting aged 42 with many infamous victories, including one over Donnie 'The Bull' Adams. His fights with Lenny 'The Guv'nor' Mclean were described by critics as among the bloodiest of the century.

He is now a very successful businessman and lives in Essex.

———————————

KATE KRAY was married to the notorious gangster Ronnie Kray. She is the bestselling author of *Diamond Geezers* (with David Bailey), *Hard Bastards* and *Hard Bastards 2, Killers* and *The Twins: Men of Violence*. She is also a top TV personality, having presented the top-rating *Hard Bastards* TV series and worked on a number of other high-profile television projects.